THE TRUTH WILL SET YOU FREE

by Michael J. Mazza

**A Presentation of the Catholic Faith
for Young Adults based on**
The Catechism of the Catholic Church

Veritas Press
PO Box 89502
Sioux Falls, SD 57105–9055
1–800–705–3367

Nihil Obstat:
    Rev. Charles Mangan, J.C.L.
    Vice–Chancellor, Diocese of Sioux Falls

Imprimatur:
    Most Rev. Bishop Paul V. Dudley, D.D.
    Sioux Falls, South Dakota
    March 19, 1995

Quotes from the Fathers of the Church in this text are from William A. Jurgen's *The Faith of the Early Fathers* series published by The Liturgical Press in Collegeville, MN in 1970. All quotes from the documents of the Second Vatican Council are from *Vatican Council II: The Conciliar and Post Conciliar Documents*, edited by Austin Flannery, O.P., and published by the Daughters of St. Paul in Boston, MA in 1987. Quotes and references from the *Catechism of the Catholic Church* come from the English translation of the *Catechism* © 1994, USCC, Inc.—Libreria Editrice Vaticana. The translation used for the Bible passages employed in this text come from the New American Bible © 1970 by the Catholic Bible Publishers, Wichita, Kansas.

Veritas Press
PO Box 89502
Sioux Falls, SD 57105–9055

Copyright © 1995, Michael J. Mazza

ISBN 0–9646214–0–1

Printed at St. Martin de Porres Printshop, New Hope, Kentucky

TABLE OF CONTENTS

Many years ago, a rich young man approached Jesus and asked him what he had to do to be saved. That same question is asked by many young people today, especially in a culture that at the same time confuses and frightens. What is the meaning of life? Why am I here? How can I be truly happy in a world full of so much pain? What will happen to me after I die?

Jesus' answer to the young man was interesting. He first invited him to keep the commandments. A tall order, indeed, but one that this particular young man had no problem keeping, apparently. "I have kept all these since my youth," he asserts. Jesus, looking at him as only God can, then gave him the key to eternal life: "Come, follow me." Jesus was telling him, in other words, that he would only be saved by wholeheartedly setting his mind and heart on cultivating a close relationship with God.

The young man, we are told, "walked away sad." No pollster was present to survey the young man's opinion of Jesus as he rode away down the road, but he was evidently disappointed in the response he got to his question, since it challenged him to radically redefine his life.

Our Lord was very good at challenging people, and he continues to do that even today through the Church he established on earth. This book is built upon the foundation of wisdom contained in the time–honored teachings of that same Catholic Church, especially as they have been expressed in the newly–released *Catechism of the Catholic Church.*

This book begins with a treatment of some of the most basic questions of life: Does God even exist? Why should I believe the Bible? Is Christ God or not, and what does it matter to me? These are important questions to which you deserve good answers. After we establish some of these basic points, we will move on to investigate the Apostles' Creed.

The Creed is not an empty formula that is meant to be muttered in church unthinkingly week after week. This short summary of Christian belief is a concise summary of life–giving truths and is an important pillar on which a truly happy life is constructed. The creed contains ideas so awesome and powerful that they have meant literally the difference between life and death for millions of young people throughout human history.

This book also seeks to help you live out these truths in your own lives. After discussing the Creed, we turn to what it means to live as a Christian in today's world by investigating the sacraments, commandments, and prayer. The sacraments are not empty ceremonies people are supposed to put up with every few years in order to have parties and receive presents, but the foundation of a strong relationship with the living God of all creation. The commandments are not abstract laws handed down by some distant deity, but the practical directions for a blessed life. Prayer, far from being something only "priests and religious do," is the intimate communication between God and his people. These, then, are the four pillars of the Catholic faith—the Creed, Sacraments, Commandments, and Prayer. They represent the fundamental ingredients for a truly happy life, and are great gifts from our loving God.

This book will challenge you. But it will also acquaint you with the truth about human existence. It will help you answer those questions human beings have faced since the beginning: What is the meaning of life? Why am I here? What is the difference between "right" and "wrong?" How can I be truly happy in this world of pain? What will happen to me after I die? There are answers to these questions, Jesus assures us. Ultimately, he himself is the answer. May you come to know Jesus the Lord better by reading and studying this book. May you grow in your relationship with the Lord who made you and who cares for you by meditating on the truths this book contains. May you come to know, by praying over this book, that Truth which alone sets us free (Jn. 8:32).

CHAPTER ONE

TRUTH OR CONSEQUENCES

Let us now begin our investigation of the Catholic Faith with one of the most basic questions of all: Does "truth" exist? In other words, can anyone say something is *objectively* true or not?

Some of you reading this book might be thinking that this is a rather obvious and perhaps even a dumb way to begin this book. But as we shall see, it is an absolutely essential question and one to which we shall turn frequently throughout the following lessons.

We know certain things are true from our **daily experience**. There is usually no dispute about statements like "this is a chair" and "that is an apple." We can also point to more sophisticated truths using our **human reason**. "Child neglect is wrong" and "parents should take care of their children" are two truths at which we very easily arrive. These truths are ingrained in us so deeply that even if we rarely think about them, we act upon them all the time. We bite into what we believe are apples all the time without sending them down to a chemistry lab beforehand for testing. Similarly, if you looked out your window right now and saw a mother beating her child with a tire iron, you would most certainly feel revulsion and would immediately try to stop her!

Despite the witness of our daily experience and basic human reason, there are some people today who deny the possibility of knowing objective truth. These people can be termed "**subjectivists**," since they claim only the individual person or "subject" decides what is true, not something or someone outside themselves that represents an objective truth to which they should conform their lives. Most often subjectivists deny objective *moral* truth, and commonly claim, "I decide for myself what is real and what is right and wrong. No one can tell *me* what to do!"

There are three main ways we may counter the subjectivists' arguments. The first is using simple **common sense**. To someone who claims one cannot know anything for certain, you simply point out an obvious reality as perceived through the senses. We can generally trust our senses to give us accurate information about our surroundings. Without this, life itself would become impossible. An honest subjectivist would never be able to eat anything unless he himself had tested it in the chemistry lab to make sure it was really food. Of course, he would then have to trust the scientific instruments he was using, too!

Another way to refute the claims of the subjectivists is to point out the **unchanging behavior of reality**. The truth of something doesn't change because of people's beliefs. It is either raining or it's not, no matter what we happen to think. The earth still revolved around the sun, even when people thought differently. If your best friend told you tomorrow that he was Napoleon Bonaparte, you would likely think he'd been hit on the head one too many times at football practice. Of course, the honest subjectivist has no way of proving or disproving whether or not your friend really is Napoleon, since subjectivists claim individuals should construct their own personal truths independent of "objective" reality.

The third and most convincing way to refute the subjectivists' claim that "there is no truth" is to point out the **inherent contradiction** of that statement. In other words, if there really is no truth, then how could a subjectivist teach that proposition as "true?" He couldn't, since that would be contradicting his whole theory. It would also be impossible for a strict subjectivist to even advance a position in an argument of any kind, since subjectivists hold that each individual makes his or her own truth. It would be obviously contradictory for subjectivists to try and convince other people that their position was "true" and that their opponent's position was "false," regardless of whether the subject was ultimate reality or the best form of defense to play against a football team with a strong running game!

Especially in the area of morality, many people today claim proudly that old moral codes are outdated, and that there are no absolute principles on which to judge actions. If you are ever confronted by someone with this idea, be sure to ask: "Are you absolutely sure that there are no absolutes?!"

Thus, since we see that subjectivism has no basis in reality, we can now safely assume truth exists. The next issue we will look at is whether or not a human soul exists, and whether we have any hope of understanding what "truth" really means.

EXERCISE #1: List what you believe to be are five objective, absolutely true statements. Prepare to defend them in a small group discussion with your fellow students.

There are two main reasons why we know human beings have souls. First, from our personal experience, we are aware that human beings have at least the **capacity for thought**. In deciding between the different nutritional values of breakfast cereals this morning, you showed that you have an intellect. You show the same power when you solve equations in algebra class. Dogs, however, do not read the labels of dog food packages to see which has less sodium, nor are they seen barking out the Pythagorean theorem!

The second reason we know human beings have souls also comes from basic human experience. Along with the capacity for rational thought, human beings also have the **capacity to make free choices**. You are free to study for your English test or cheat off of someone else. Whichever path you choose, however, you must live with the consequences of your free actions. No other living thing in creation shares that awesome power. Can you see a farmer "grounding" one his young bulls for staying out too late with the pretty heifer three stalls down? Do we see ducks on "the Peoples' Court?" Of course not! Animals are not responsible for things the way we are, since they are not human beings with free wills.

Precisely because we have the capacity to think and choose freely, we have an important dignity. While we may not stir at seeing an elderly gentleman walking his dog on a leash, we might become upset if he had his *wife* on a leash! It is beneath the dignity of a human being to be treated in such a fashion, since human beings have rational "souls," this great capacity for thinking and choosing, whereas animals and plants do not.

So far we have established two main points. Since we have shown that truth exists, we can now at least be open to seeing what this "truth" is. Second, we have been assured that we have the ability to perform this task because of our intellect and will, the two "operations" of the human soul. Only now can we turn to a discussion about whether or not God exists.

CHAPTER TWO

DOES GOD EXIST?

The Catholic Church teaches that God's existence can be known with certainty through the right use of reason, though this knowledge is limited and imperfect. Many different "proofs" for the existence of God have been used throughout the centuries. Dr. Peter Kreeft, a philosophy professor at Boston College and a convert to Catholicism, has assembled five basic reasons why it is reasonable to believe in God in his book *Fundamentals of the Faith* (San Francisco: Ignatius Press, 1988). We will now look at each of these five reasons as well as the main objection to God's existence posed by people today.

REASON #1: FIRST CAUSE ARGUMENT

This is probably the most common argument used against atheists, even though most people are unaware it is called by this name. It is obvious from our human experience that everything must have a cause. If, when you go home tonight, you find a brand new Ferrari in your garage, you would probably assume 1) it is a stolen vehicle, 2) you're hallucinating, or 3) your parents are being extra generous this Christmas. You would not assume it just popped out of nothingness. In the same way, we can ask where everything came from, if not from God.

According to this argument, there must be a "first cause" which has caused everything else to come into being. This first cause must be "**independent**;" that is, without a source itself. It must also be "**necessary**;" that is, it must always have existed and *cannot not exist*, just as a triangle cannot not have three sides.

Some people claim that the universe was created with a "big bang" out of primal matter floating around in space. This very well might have happened, but it certainly does not disprove God's existence. God could have started things off any way He wished! Besides, one may ask, where did the "primal matter" come from? Or who or what provided the "spark" for the big bang?

REASON #2: THE ARGUMENT FROM DESIGN

This argument is even clearer than the first one. We know from our experience that where there is design, there must be a designer. Say, for example, you were on a search mission in the Pacific for survivors from a shipwreck. You fly over a deserted island and see the letters "H–E–L–P" written in the sand. Do you head for home, remarking how coincidental it was for the wind to arrange the sand in that fashion? Of course not! You radio the rescue team, knowing that where there is design (the sign in the sand), there must be a designer (the survivor who arranged it). The next step in the argument claims that there is design in the universe. This is rather obvious, since everything from the capillaries in your little finger to the human brain to the solar system show very clearly certain complex patterns of design. Therefore, this argument concludes, there must be a designer of the universe.

Some may claim the theory of evolution explains the design behind creation, and thus excludes the idea of "God." Again, this theory (and it is still just a theory), may well be true. God could have brought higher species into being in any manner He wanted to. If one fails to acknowledge God's guidance over the evolutionary process, however, it is as ridiculous as believing watches could assemble themselves, and that pieces of metal have miraculously hurled themselves together in an intricate pattern on millions of wrists around the world. Yet believing that watches put themselves together is more reasonable than believing the entire *universe* put itself together, which consists of billions of not only watches, but waterfalls, woodchucks, watermelons, and wrists, not to mention the people to whom they are attached!

A short story might help illustrate this point. An atheist once visited the classroom of his old science teacher, a believer in God. The former noticed a model of the solar system on the latter's desk and asked where he had purchased it. "Oh, I didn't buy it," said the teacher, "it just pieced itself together out of thin air." "Very funny," replied the atheist, "but seriously, where did it come from?" The scientist replied, "If you believe the real solar system pieced itself together, why can't you believe the same thing about a $5 model I got at a drugstore?"

REASON #3: ARGUMENT FROM CONSCIENCE

Most people would agree that a person's conscience could be described as that place in your heart from which you make judgments about right and wrong. Further, most people would agree that some kind of objective morality does exist in the consciences of every human being. For example, it is inconceivable that any human being could ever think vicious abuse of children would be pardonable, or that shooting people for no other reason than because they have blonde hair is a good thing. The question we can ask, then, is this: "Where does this objective morality come from, if not from God?" We will now examine four very common attempts to answer this question.

One common response is that our sense of right and wrong come not from God, but from a **"little voice"** in our heads. This might work occasionally, but it totally depends on whose "voice" it is. Even psychotic killers have said "little voices" told them to kill their victims. We must, therefore, have more to base our judgments on than simply "little voices."

Another way of explaining the origins of objective morality exclusive of God is by saying that right and wrong is a **biological instinct or "gut feeling."** Yet human beings have many instincts, and at times we have to suppress them or choose one over the other. For example, suppose you were out on a dinner date for the first time with someone on whom you have a huge crush. The dish you order turns out to look and smell like last week's trash. Your date's meal, however, appears delicious. Do you check your instinct to eat or do you leap across the table and stuff your date's dish in your mouth? You suppress the instinct to eat your date's meal because it would be socially suicidal and morally wrong to do so in that situation. Instincts alone cannot explain the inalienable and undeniable authority of conscience.

The same is true of feelings. It is a common experience for a high school age student to fall madly in love with someone who is outwardly attractive. But it often happens that the feelings cool considerably after you get to know the person better and realize they have faults like everyone else. The same person you thought you wanted to marry one week ago you can't stand sitting next to in history class! Feelings come and go, and cannot alone explain how we come to these strong beliefs we possess in our consciences.

The third attempt for explaining how we know right from wrong without including God goes like this: "Moral norms are **dictated by the society** in which you live." This is quite a strong argument and works well much of the time, yet there are some notable exceptions which show its limits. Was it "good" or "moral" to cooperate with the Nazis as they attempted to exterminate the Jews in the 1930s? Were the apartheid laws in South Africa "good," just because "society" said so? What about abortion in the United States? Is the murder of innocent children "right" because a handful of Supreme Court justices declared it to be so in 1973? It should be clear, then, that merely claiming "society" tells us what is right and wrong will not be enough.

The last and most popular method of explaining what is right and wrong without mentioning God and objective morality is by saying "**as long as it doesn't hurt anyone**, it is morally permissible." The first question we can ask is this: "Where did you get the idea that 'hurting anyone' was something to be avoided?" That sounds like an objective principle of morality. Secondly, you can point out that this theory gives a stamp of approval to such acts as bestiality, consensual incest, and even cannibalism! After all, what is wrong (according to this theory) with running down to the morgue for a late night snack, since the people are dead anyway? You're not "hurting anyone!"

Thus, we see that the only real basis upon which we can decide that certain actions are right and certain other actions are wrong rests with the Creator, the Being Who made us. *God* must be the only source for objective morality and the consciences we all possess.

EXERCISE #2: With one other partner, write out an imaginary dialogue between a believer and an atheist. Outline as many of the atheists' arguments as you can and then refute them.

REASON #4: ARGUMENT FROM HISTORY

The argument from history, while not as strictly logical as the first three, is very important for many people. It essentially states that God's actions have been seen throughout human history, and thus point very clearly to His existence. This argument has three main parts: Israel, the Church, and miracles.

First of all, history relates to us that a particular group of people called "Israel" claimed to be specially chosen by God, who brought them out of the bonds of slavery and made of them a great nation. If God does not exist, this argument asks, were Moses, the prophets, the kings, and all the Jews lying or simply mistaken? Of course, either is a possibility, but is it *likely*?

Similarly, human history shows a group of people calling themselves the "New Israel;" that is, the Christians. If there really is no God, then have all the Christians of all time just been fooled? How could the Church have lasted for so long if it was merely a human institution?

Third, the abundance of miracles that have occurred throughout the ages must at least give pause to an honest searcher. If there is no God, then how can we explain the many miracles that have happened for which there has been no scientific explanation?

For one example, let us turn to the miraculous blood of St. Januarius. Januarius was the bishop of Beneventum in the early church who suffered martyrdom during a persecution by the Roman Emperor Diocletian around the year 305 A.D. Some early Christians gathered up his remains after he had been beheaded, and reportedly collected some of his blood into two small flasks. These flasks were eventually placed in a sealed reliquary behind two glass plates. Since the 14th century, it is reported that on certain feast days throughout the year the liquid inside one of the flasks liquifies and bubbles, changing from a dark mass of what appears to be dried blood to a red fluid flowing freely inside the flask. The apparent miracle occurs in both cold and hot weather and when attended to by large crowds or in the presence of only a few spectators. A spectrometer test in 1902 revealed the substance to be blood, and when the reliquary was weighed in more tests a few years later, tests showed that both the volume and the weight of the fluid appear to change dramatically, and unexplainably, before and after the liquification occurs.

Another example of an scientifically–unexplainable miracle comes from the story of a French woman named Madame Biré, who had lost her sight in February of 1908 due to the fact her optic nerve, which "carries" images from the eye to the brain, had withered. A few months later, she went to visit Lourdes, a small town in France where the Virgin Mary had reportedly appeared to a peasant girl in 1858. At 10:15am on August 5, 1908, after having received Holy Communion at the morning Mass and just as the Blessed Sacrament was being carried in procession in front of her, Madame Biré regained her sight. A doctor immediately examined her, and found that not only had her vision been completely restored, but that her optic nerve was still withered. A few months later, a team of doctors found that her optic nerve had been completely healed and restored. This miracle is documented at the Medical Bureau at Lourdes and can be investigated by anyone who wishes to do so.

Yet another example of a modern miracle that shows the hand of God in human affairs is what happened at Fatima, Portugal, on October 13, 1917. The Blessed Virgin Mary had been reportedly appearing to three shepherd children in a field on a regular basis during the preceding months. The day before the last anticipated apparition, the eldest child, Lucia, predicted that a miracle would occur shortly after noon. A crowd of skeptics and believers totalling 70,000 people assembled in the

Cova da Iria the following day. Shortly after noon, a sign did appear. The sun began to whirl around in the sky, shooting out rays of different color light. Suddenly, the sun seemed to become detached from its orbit and began to fall to the earth. Observers thought it was the end of the world. All at once, however, the sun returned to the sky. This event was recorded by all the several newspapers in the world, and defies natural explanation.

Someone who does not believe in God or claims we can know nothing about Him is hard pressed to answer the questions posed by these and the many other supernatural occurrences that have happened throughout human history.

REASON #5: PASCAL'S WAGER

Pascal's Wager is named after a French mathematician and Catholic philosopher in the 17th century. This argument is not strictly logical, either, but it helps a great many people to at least contemplate the possibility of God's existence who otherwise normally would not even consider it. Blaise Pascal was distressed by the carelessness with which many of his scientific colleagues were dismissing religion at the dawn of the scientific age. Many of them thought belief in God was obsolescent, now that mankind had "found all the answers" with science. In response, Pascal proposed his famous "wager."

All of us, Pascal stated, are each day growing closer to death. Because of this inescapable reality, all of us are called upon to choose whether or not we believe in God and an afterlife. Say, for example, Becky decides to believe in God. Tom, on the other hand, decides to bet that God does not exist. If Tom is right, then both Becky and Tom will end up in the same state—six feet under the earth in their respective coffins. If Becky is right, however, and has lived her life in accord with that hope, she has the possibility of enjoying the eternal life God has promised. Tom, however, faces the certain possibility of spending eternity separated from God. Becky cannot lose, and Tom cannot win. The best choice, then, according to Pascal, was to wager and live as if God existed. While not offering the best reason to believe in God, Pascal's Wager does make some people sit up and listen to the claims of revealed religion.

Thus far we have covered five reasons why it is reasonable to believe in God. Many people who can intellectually accept this, however, still do not admit to a belief in God. This is due in large measure to **the problem of evil**. In this final part of this chapter on God's existence, we will deal with the problems raised by the question: "How can a good God exist who allows so much evil in the world?" This question is often asked by

MOTHER OF SORROWS
PRAY FOR US

Quis non posset contristari,
Piam Matrem contemplari
Dolentem cum Filio?
Who could fail to grieve,
Seeing the Blessed Mother
suffering with her Son?

– from the Stabat Mater (Suffering Mother),
a 13th century Franciscan poem

people who are truly hurting over some painful experience they have had, and their apparent rejection of God does not come so much from firm philosophical convictions, but out of a wounded heart. People in this situation need our care and compassion, and it would be unfair to simply label them as "dumb" or "sinful" because they cannot yet define their belief in God.

Having said this, we still have an obligation to present the truth charitably and prudently to those who seek it. With regard to the objection at hand, the first thing we must keep in mind here is that God did not make evil. He freely, out of love, made all things good. Yet, as we saw before, God also gave us a free will with which we can reject or accept Him. All evil is directly or indirectly the result of free will choices made by sinful human beings to sin (cf. CCC, #400). God loves us and respects us too much to constantly violate our free will by "running down from heaven" every time someone is about to use their free will and do something sinful. That would mean we were not truly free!

Some may ask at this point: "Well, if God knew that human beings would misuse the gift of free will, why did He give it to us then?" The answer is surprisingly easy—because *perfect love must be free*. How would you feel if you were forced to go on your next date at gunpoint? How about marrying someone because you were literally forced to? Such scenes make us uncomfortable, since our love in those situations would not be true since it was not freely given. God invites us to love Him perfectly, but in order to do so He must leave us free to reject Him.

Many people today ask the question: "If God is so good, why do bad things happen to good people?" Although this is a very important question, there are three questionable assumptions inherent in it. First, it might be a bit arrogant for us to *demand* that the Almighty God tell us the many reasons He allows certain things to happen. If He lets us know the reason somehow, that is fine. We may even ask for this in prayer. But God is never *obligated* to give us creatures anything, and certainly knows what is best for us in the long run.

Another important assumption this question makes is that all suffering is without value. This is certainly not the case. You would never succeed in sports if you never worked hard in practice. The pain felt after a good workout is often a necessary part of building up one's muscles. On a little higher level, Mother Teresa has recounted several times how even the terrible disease of AIDS can bring about great good. Some of her patients have reconciled themselves to God or to their families in the last days afforded to them. This has turned out to be a great blessing, and one that would have been missed had the person died suddenly in a car crash rather than through AIDS.

The third major assumption this question contains is that there are "good" people who deserve only "good" things. This is quite a claim, considering the obvious fact that no human being is "good" compared to God the Creator, and that anything we enjoy, be it water, air, or life itself is a free gift of God to which we have no absolute right. No one created him or herself or ordered God to make him or her on a particular day, and so we should be extremely careful about *ordering* God to give us "good" things.

Jumping ahead a bit to Christian revelation, we could also remember that God never leaves us alone in suffering. God did not become man to take away our sufferings right away, but to share in them, give a profound meaning to them, and by means of them make possible for us the kingdom of heaven.

Thus we finally arrive at the end of our third chapter. Having hopefully grasped why it is reasonable to believe in God, we will now look at the one religion which claims it is the one He Himself became man to establish and wants all peoples to adhere to.

EXERCISE #3: Answer the following questions and discuss in class. Which of the five reasons to believe in God do you find most helpful, if any? Why?

CHAPTER THREE

THE RELIABILITY OF THE GOSPELS

Having hopefully grasped why it is reasonable to believe in God, we will now look at the one religion which claims it is the one He himself became man to establish and wants all peoples to adhere to. The first step in examining the claims of Christianity is looking at its written accounts of the life of its Founder, Jesus Christ. The claims of these four "gospels" are central to the truth of the Christian religion, so it is important to briefly examine whether or not the gospels are even reliable at all. In order to do this, we shall use four criteria that are used to judge virtually any supposedly historical work: Do we really have an accurate text? Is the information in the text supported by other sources? Were the texts written by first–hand observers? Did the authors stand to gain in some way from writing so that their objectivity might be compromised?

CRITERIA #1: Do we have accurate texts?

It is an unfortunate fact of human history that we have no "autographed" original manuscripts of ancient documents. Most likely lost for all time due to the effects of age and weather, every ancient document we have, from the writings of Plato to the historical works of Thucydides, has come down to us only in the form of copies typically written at least 800 years after the original. Although the human community at this point does not have any original "autographed" copies of the ancient manuscripts of the Gospels, either, the copies of the Gospels we do have are much older than any other ancient document. Furthermore, a 1976 survey showed that there exist over 5,000 early texts of New Testament writings, either fragments or whole manuscripts, all of which are written in the original Greek. No other ancient document comes close to having that many copies in existence; none have over 1,000 copies.

The oldest copies of the entire New Testament we have date back to about the middle of the 4th century A.D. One copy, the **Vatican Codex**, is stored in the Vatican Library while the other, discovered in 1844 in the monastery of St. Catherine on Mt. Sinai, is known as the **Sinai Codex** and is currently housed in the British Library. The **Bodmer Papyri** contain parts of Luke and John and date to about the year A.D. 200. The oldest piece of Scripture we have, dating back to the year 135 A.D., is called the **Rylands Papyrus 457**, and contains four verses from the 18th chapter of St. John's Gospel. What is even more remarkable about these manuscripts is that they substantially agree with each other, which enables us to reasonably conclude they convey certain basic facts about the life of Jesus.

CRITERIA #2: Is the information supported by other sources?

An important step in the proof of the reliability of any work claiming to be historical is searching to find if the information the work contains has been verified by any other outside source. The basic information contained in the Gospels has indeed been verified by reliable outside sources.

Flavius Josephus, a first century Romanized Jewish historian, noted in his famous work *Antiquities of the Jews* (7.2.3) that Jesus lived, performed miracles, had a large following, was crucified, and had reportedly risen from the dead. This information is quite significant, since it comes from a reputable historian and from someone who was not a Christian.

The same is true of **Tacitus**, a Roman historian especially noted for his accurate reporting, who noted the execution of Christ "during the reign of Tiberius, by the procurator Pontius Pilate" (*Annals*, 15.44). Thus, the Gospel accounts of Jesus' crucifixion are supported by this non–Christian source.

Another non–Christian source that indirectly supports the Gospel accounts of Jesus' performance of miracles are the **Pharisees**, that group of Jews who deeply resented Christ. In Luke 11:14–20, we see the Pharisees attacking Jesus, claiming that He was performing signs with the help of Satan. Jesus simply points out the obvious contradiction in their argument, noting that if it is by Satan He expels Satan from people, Satan's kingdom could not last. The interesting thing about this passage is that the Pharisees do not dispute that a miracle occurred. They simply cannot or do not want to admit the fact that Jesus performed miracles through the power of God.

CRITERIA #3: Were the texts written by first–hand observers?

St. Irenaeus, a bishop of Lyons (in what is now France) who was martyred in about the year A.D. 200, mentioned in his great work *Against Heresies* (3.1.1) that St. Matthew wrote a gospel in Hebrew; St. Mark, St. Peter's interpreter, wrote a gospel based on what Peter, his mentor, had been preaching in Rome; and that St. Luke wrote a gospel based on St. Paul's preaching.

While some of the exact dates for original authorship of the Bible are still under discussion in the scholastic community, the latest dates generally given for the "synoptic" gospels (Matthew, Mark, and Luke) are around A.D. 80, well within the lifetime of eyewitnesses to Jesus Christ. The Gospel of St. John was likely written at the end of the apostle's life, around the years A.D. 90–100.

CRITERIA #4: Did the authors have anything to gain?

Since being noted as a Christian in the early centuries often meant being marked for death, we can reasonably conclude that the gospel writers were not trying to make the best sellers' list in the local bookstores in Palestine. Not only did most of them lose their lives for the gospel, but they also knew the eternal salvation of their own souls and the souls of all those who would read their accounts were at stake, so it is reasonable to assume they would have worked very hard to make sure they got their facts straight.

Based on these four criteria, therefore, we can safely claim that the Gospels are at the very least reliable historical documents written by honest eyewitnesses that contain certain basic information about Jesus. We will examine just what that basic information is in the next chapter.

FOUR BASIC FACTS ABOUT JESUS CHRIST

Having shown that the Gospels are reliable historical accounts, let us now turn to four basic facts they can tell us about the life of Christ. (For a fuller examination of the "basic facts about Jesus," see the book *Catholic Apologetics Today* by Fr. William A. Most.)

FACT #1: There was a man named Jesus who claimed to be sent from God.

The fact that a man named Jesus lived in 1st century Palestine is obvious, as is the statement that He claimed to be sent from God. The historically reliable documents of Scripture show repeatedly that Jesus claimed to be sent by God (see Matthew 5–7; Mark 14:62; Luke 4:17– 24; John 5:30, 7:16; et. al.). No one seriously doubts this most basic fact.

FACT #2: He performed enough miracles to prove His claim.

Noting the important role miracles play in substantiating the claims of Christianity is as important as it is delicate. Some apparently miraculous events may only be coincidences, natural healings, or cures by the power of suggestion. Given the fact that people outside Christianity have also been shown to perform apparent miracles, we seem to be opening ourselves up to an empty argument. There is, however, an important distinction between the miracles of Christ and these other signs.

Jesus' miracles were generally performed to prove a particular claim. For example, when responding to the question of John the Baptist about whether or not He was "the one who is to come," Jesus responds by pointing to His miracles that show His authenticity and authority. In John 10:25 and Mt. 11:3–5, Jesus clearly states that His miracles testify to

Him. Also, in the story of the raising of Jairus' daughter from the dead in Mark 5:21–43, Jesus urges the family to have faith and the child will be well. He then enters the house and brings the little girl back to life. In Matthew 9:27–29, Jesus asks the two blind men who are asking Him for a cure if they believe He could cure them. When they respond affirmatively, He replies: "Let it be done for you according to your faith." Yet another example of this phenomena is found in the story of the cure of the paralytic. In Luke 5:17–26, Jesus first forgives the paralytic's sins, since healing the soul is much more important than in just healing the body. After all, in a few years, the man would be dead and unable to use his legs anyway. Jesus was thus giving Him an incredible gift; an opportunity for eternal life with God. Still, the Pharisees reacted angrily. In order to prove that He had authority on earth to forgive sins, He cured the man of his physical ailment right then and there. This is one of the clearest examples in the Gospels of a miracle being used to establish a tie between the miracle and the claim.

FACT #3: He chose a smaller group of followers with whom He shared more.

It would stand to reason that a leader of a movement would seek to perpetuate it by forming leaders who would take over after the founder moved on. Thus, we should not be surprised to see Jesus doing just this at several points in the Gospels: Matthew 17:1–8; Mark 4:11; Luke 6:12–16; John 17:6–19; et. al.

FACT #4: He ordered them to teach and assured them that God would protect them from error.

Again, it only stands to reason that Jesus would send out some of His followers to spread His message. In many places in the Gospels, we see Jesus commissioning His apostles: Mark 3:13–14; Matthew 28:19–20; Luke 10:16; et. al. He also promises them that the Holy Spirit will protect them from error so that the People of God would not be led astray: Matthew 16:16–19, 18:17–18; John 16:12–15, 21:15–17, et. al.

Having established the fact that Jesus Christ instituted a Church which He guaranteed would be free from error when teaching in matters of faith and morals, we can now safely turn to this teaching authority for answers to the very tough but absolutely crucial questions posed by modern living.

Let us examine how far we have come in these first five chapters. Having first established the reality of objective truth and the human soul, we then learned five very sound reasons why belief in God is reasonable. Next, we identified the reasons why we could trust, at the very least, the historical information the four Christian Gospels give us. The objective data contained in those Gospels show us, again at the very least, a holy man performing amazing miracles that proved He was from God, and that He set up an infallible teaching authority that would guide His Church community to all truth and protect them from error. Thus, we now turn to the role of the pope in the life of the Church.

EXERCISE #4: Copy, word for word, some of the pertinent Scripture passages mentioned in this lesson, identifying each with one of the four basic facts about Jesus: Matthew 11:3–5, 16:16–19, 28:19–20; Luke 10:16; John 10:25; and Mark 4:11.

CHAPTER FIVE

THE PAPACY

The Church has always taught that the "Holy Father," as the pope is called, plays a very important role in the Church, the family of God on earth. Papal **"primacy"** means that the pope is the supreme head of the Catholic Church, ruling the faithful in the place of Christ. Papal **"infallibility,"** meanwhile, means the pope, as supreme teacher of the faithful, cannot teach error in matters of faith and morals. If you were infallible in geometry, for example, it would mean you would be prevented from putting down any wrong answers on any geometry test, just as the Pope is prevented from teaching error in matters of faith and morals because of divine grace.

It is important to note here that this doctrine does *not* mean several things. The belief in papal infallibility does not extend to the Pope's personal opinions (e.g., the weather or sports scores), nor does it extend to matters of Church discipline (disciplining disobedient clergy, investing Church money, receiving certain political figures, etc.) Nor does it protect what is said in private audiences, what he wrote or said before he became pope, or when he speaks as a private theologian or in regard to private revelations. Further, papal infallibility does not guarantee the pope will be particularly courageous or clear when he writes or speaks officially, but only *that he will not teach error.*

Papal infallibility does not mean impeccability, which is being without sin. See Galatians 2:11–16 for the story of how St. Peter was rightly, though respectfully, reprimanded by St. Paul for his lack of courage and for not living out his true teaching. It is a sad fact that popes can, have, and do sin, some grievously so. What is remarkable, however, is that no pope, no matter how sinful, has ever taught error in matters of faith and morals as the supreme teacher of the faithful.

The Church teaches that papal infallibility is exercised in two ways: through the extraordinary and ordinary Magisterium. "**Magisterium**" is the term describing the living "teaching authority" of the Church. The **extraordinary** Magisterium consists of solemn declarations by the pope himself or through certain official statements of a papally–approved general council of bishops. Pope Pius XII's 1950 definition of Mary's Assumption and the First Vatican Council's teaching on papal infallibility fall under this category. **Ordinary** Magisterium is what is clearly and consistently taught by the pope in "encyclicals" (special letters from the pope) and other official statements. Just because an issue has not been solemnly defined through extraordinary magisterium, it does not mean the issue is then "up for grabs." Many very basic Christian truths have never been solemnly defined by the pope himself, but still belong to that basic set of truths which must be believed by all Christians.

Pope Pius XII, in his 1950 encyclical *Humani Generis*, taught this very same point in paragraph #20 when he wrote that

> nor must it be thought that what is expounded in Encyclical Letters does not of itself demand consent, since in writing such Letters the Popes do not exercise the supreme power of their Teaching Authority. For these matters are taught with the ordinary teaching authority, of which it is true to say: "He who heareth you, heareth me" (Luke 10:16); and generally what is expounded and inculcated in Encyclical Letters already for other reasons appertains to Catholic doctrine. But if the Supreme Pontiffs in their official documents purposely pass judgment on a matter up to that time under dispute, it is obvious that that matter, according to the mind and will of the same Pontiffs, cannot be any longer considered a question open to discussion among theologians.

We will now look at several historical examples that show Christians have believed in this primacy of the pope since the beginning. St. Clement of Rome, the fourth Bishop of Rome or "pope," intervened in a schism that had divided the Christian community at Corinth around the year A.D. 95. He speaks as one with authority to settle the dispute, even though it is not within his diocese, and claims: "If anyone disobey the things which have been said by Him (Jesus) through us, let them know that they will involve themselves in transgression and in no small danger" (*Letter to the Corinthians*, [59,1]). This claim would be arrogant and tyrannical if it were not made by someone who was given that kind of authority over the Church by God Himself, and would have surely been resisted by the early Church.

Another historical example that shows the people in the early Church really did acknowledge the supremacy of the pope can be seen in the work *Against Heresies*, written by St. Irenaeus of Lyons around the years A.D. 180–199. In Book III, section 3.2, he gives us a list of popes, the oldest such list now known to exist, and points out

> the successions of the bishops of the most ancient Church known to all, founded and organized at Rome by the two most glorious Apostles, Peter and Paul, that Church which has the tradition and the faith which comes down to us after having been announced to men by the Apostles. For with this Church, because of its superior origin, all Churches must agree, that is, all the faithful in the whole world; and it is in her that the faithful everywhere have maintained the Apostolic tradition.

Throughout the early centuries of Christianity, many saints (St. Cyprian of Carthage, St. Augustine, St. Cyril of Jerusalem, St. Ephraim, Pope St. Damasus I, et. al.) and Church councils (e.g., Ephesus and Chalcedon) upheld this teaching of papal primacy. In 1274, the Second Council of Lyons defined that "the holy Roman Church holds the supreme and full primacy over the whole Catholic Church, together with fullness of power, which it truly and humbly recognizes it received from the Lord Himself in blessed Peter, prince and summit of the Apostles, whose successor is the Roman Pontiff." (DS 861)

In 1870, the First Vatican Council defined the doctrine of papal infallibility in its document *Pastor Aeternus*. It should be clear that "defining" a doctrine does not mean "inventing" it, but rather that the Church sets down in writing a belief that had generally been taken for granted for a period of time. Much like how the ground rules for a pickup basketball game have to be vocally agreed upon only after the first conflict, the Church usually only defines those things which have lately come under dispute or attack. Vatican I taught that it was

> a divinely revealed dogma that the Roman Pontiff, when he speaks *ex cathedra*, that is, when functioning as the pastor and teacher of all Christians, by his supreme Apostolic authority he defines a doctrine on faith or morals to be held by the whole Church, through the divine assistance promised him in blessed Peter, enjoys that infallibility with which the divine Redeemer willed His Church should be equipped in defining a doctrine of faith or morals, and so, that such definitions of the Roman Pontiff are irreformable, of themselves and not from the consent of the Church (DS 3073–3075).

Finally, the most recent general council of the Church, Vatican II, completed the work of Vatican I on papal primacy and infallibility. Bishops from all over the world assembled in Rome during the years 1962–65 to discuss how the Church could be a more effective instrument in the hand of God during the modern age. To this end, the bishops wrote a series of documents, which were approved by Pope Paul VI. In paragraph #25 of its rich document on the Church *Lumen Gentium*, the bishops at Vatican II claim:

> Bishops who teach in communion with the Roman Pontiff are to be revered by all as witnesses of divine and Catholic truth; the faithful, for their part, are obliged to submit to their bishops' decision, made in the name of Christ, in matters of faith and morals, and to adhere to it with a ready and respectful allegiance of mind. This loyal submission of the will and intellect must be given, in a special way, to the authentic teaching authority of the Roman Pontiff, even when he does not speak *ex cathedra* [meaning "from the chair" or "officially"] in such wise, indeed, that his supreme teaching authority be acknowledged with respect, and that one sincerely adhere to decisions made by him, conformably with his manifest mind and intention, which is made known principally either by the character of the documents in question, or by the frequency with which a certain doctrine is proposed, or by the manner in which the doctrine is formulated... This infallibility, however, with which the divine redeemer wished to endow his Church in defining doctrine pertaining to faith and morals, is co–extensive with the deposit of revelation, which must be religiously guarded and loyally and courageously expounded. The Roman Pontiff, head of the college of bishops, enjoys this infallibility in virtue of his office, when, as supreme pastor and teacher of all the faithful—who confirms his brethren in their faith (see Luke 22:32)—he proclaims in an absolute decision a doctrine pertaining to faith or morals. For that reason his definitions are rightly said to be irreformable by their very nature and not by reason of the assent of the Church, in as much as they were made with the assistance of the Holy Spirit promised to him in the person of blessed Peter himself; and as a consequence they are in no way in need of the approval of others, and do not admit of appeal to any other tribunal. For in such a case the Roman Pontiff does not utter a pronouncement as a private person, but rather does he expound and defend the teaching of the Catholic faith as the supreme teacher of the universal Church, in whom the Church's charism of infallibility is present in a singular way.

All these historical arguments are meant to prove that the Church has always taught the importance of the doctrines of papal primacy and of papal infallibility. Though much misunderstood today, the Church's teaching on the papacy is especially important and a great gift Christ has given His Church. It is no small matter that one of the pope's titles is the Vicar of Christ. "Vicar" is Latin for "substitute," and so we can rightly claim the pope is Christ's "substitute teacher" on earth. Through the Supreme Pontiff (another title of the pope which literally means "bridge builder"), Christ is able to keep order within the household of the family of God.

EXERCISE #5: In your journal, answer the following question: What do you think the Church would be like if the pope were not infallible when teaching in matters of faith and morals?

THE APOSTLES' CREED

(from the *Catechism of the Catholic Church*, pp. 49–50)

1. I believe in God, the Father almighty, creator of heaven and earth;
2. and in Jesus Christ, his only Son, our Lord.
3. He was conceived by the power of the Holy Spirit, and was born of the Virgin Mary.
4. He suffered under Pontius Pilate, was crucified, died, and was buried.
5. He descended into hell. On the third day he rose again.
6. He ascended into heaven and is seated at the right hand of the Father.
7. He will come again to judge the living and the dead.
8. I believe in the Holy Spirit,
9. the holy catholic Church, the communion of saints,
10. the forgiveness of sins,
11. the resurrection of the body,
12. and life everlasting. Amen.

"You call me 'teacher' and 'master,' and rightly so, for indeed I am" (John 13:13).

CHAPTER SIX

KEEPING THE FAITH

The Apostles' Creed is so named because it dates back to the time of the apostles and the very early Church. It was then and still is now a required part of the initiation rites of all converts to the Catholic Faith. It has been divided up into twelve articles, which we will examine one by one in the chapters that follow.

You might have noticed that the Apostles' Creed differs somewhat from another popular creed you might be used to hearing at Sunday Mass called the "Nicene" Creed. That statement of belief, while based on the Apostles' Creed, goes into more depth on certain issues because of the historical situation in which it was written. In the 4th century, various people were questioning certain basic Christian doctrines (Christ's divinity, the Holy Trinity, etc.). In response, both the Council of Nicea (325) and the First Council of Constantinople (381) elaborated a bit on the basic information contained in the Apostles' Creed and thus the Nicene Creed was born. We shall be looking at this "younger sister" of the Apostles' Creed a bit later.

The creed begins with the words **"I believe"**. In Latin, that is written "Credo," which is where we get the word "creed." The act of believing is an *act of faith*. There are two types of faith: **natural faith** and **supernatural faith**.

Natural faith is having confidence in things and/or trusting people. It is a normal and essential part of life, and something that we use all the time. For example, we generally trust what our parents, teachers, map makers, and newscasters say or there would be massive confusion. When you open a map, you have confidence that what it shows is true, and you trust the people who made the map are telling the truth, even though you may have never met them.

Supernatural faith, on the other hand, is believing in what God has told us about Himself. It is a free gift to all those who seek it (see He-

27

brews 11:6), the means by which we begin to live with God (see John 17:3), and the means by which God gives a right direction to our present life (see Hab. 2:4).

The creed next speaks of believing **"in God"**. We have already spoken of five good reasons why belief in God is reasonable. Besides that basic information, God has revealed Himself through the sources of Revelation as a "Triune" God. In other words, the one God is an eternal community of three Divine "Persons," separate yet fundamentally equal, all of whom have always existed and always will exist, who live in a constant exchange of love. It is important to note that the word "person," when used in the description of this mystery, does not mean exactly the same thing as we commonly use it today. Among the Persons of the Blessed Trinity, there are not three separate wills or intellects. This "Mystery of the Holy Trinity," though it does not contradict reason, goes well beyond the capacity of our limited human intellects. We hope and pray that we will one day not only come to a better understanding of this awesome truth, but that we will actually share in the life of this heavenly society.

Returning to the creed, we come upon the short phrase **"the Father almighty"** and recognize it means a great deal. It serves as a summary for all the "attributes" or characteristics of God the Church has taught we can know from both natural reason (using our own minds) and by revelation (listening to what God actually tells us about Himself). God is "almighty" in that he is omnipotent (all–powerful), omniscient (all–knowing), omnipresent (always present), eternal (not restricted by the limits of time), perfect (unchanging), transcendent (totally above us and worthy of awe and holy fear), pure spirit (not dependent on any matter), one (unique), and all– good, to name a few of God's "attributes."

When Jesus told people to call God "Father" (Matthew 6:9), He must have really shocked some of His hearers. While God had been referred to as "Father" in the Old Testament, it was relatively rare. Jesus' actual word "Abba" meant something like our word "Daddy" does now. Our Lord really wanted people to know how much God the Father really does love us and just how close He wants to be to us, His "children."

EXERCISE #6: Answer the following reflection question in your journal: 1) List five times in the past week when you have shown natural faith and, if applicable, five times you have displayed supernatural faith.

The fact that God is **"creator of heaven and earth"** is testified to in Scripture (see Rom. 1:19–20). We also know that He made everything "good" (see Gen. 1:31). We further know from the Nicene Creed that He made "all that is seen and unseen." This means, as the *Catechism of the*

Catholic Church teaches, that God made angels first and then man.

Angels are "unseen" and purely spiritual beings. They are not plump little naked cherubs with harps and wings. Those are simply artistic images that we have inherited from years past. Though they do not possess bodies, they are real and living persons who, like us, have intellects and free wills. The Church teaches that at the beginning of time, some of these angels, using their free wills, rebelled against God and thus chose to leave heaven.

These "devils" still exist, and are in engaged in a constant attempt to foil God's loving plan. The chief devil, "Lucifer," (also known as "Satan") though he will never be victorious, can inflict very serious damage upon the world, especially when people wittingly or unwittingly cooperate with him. Some angels, thankfully, did not abuse their free will and have come to play a special part in God's saving plan. The Church teaches that all of us have guardian angels, who guard us into right paths if we but ask for their help and guidance (see Mt. 18:10).

After His creation of the angels, God made the first human pair. In the creation story in Genesis 2–3, the name "Adam" means "man," and the name "Eve" is derived from a Hebrew verb and means "mother of all the living." This first human pair were given some extraordinarily wonderful gifts by God. First, they were able to think clearly and choose freely. Second, they were able to live forever without pain of any kind. Third, they were able to live in God's presence, in what was essentially a "heaven on earth." Besides giving them all these gifts, God also gave them the freedom to accept or reject Him. As you probably are well aware, they chose to reject Him by committing some kind of sin of prideful disobedience. This is what is called "original sin," since it affected mankind at its origins.

The effects of this sin were enormous. First, because they had misused the gifts of intellect and will God have given them, they lost their ability to think clearly and choose freely. This is similar to the case of a young boy who misuses a birthday gift. Instead of using his brand new baseball bat outside on the field, he uses it as a weapon against his little sister! His parents would most certainly take the gift away until he can learn to use it in the way it was supposed to be used. Second, since Adam and Eve had pridefully rejected the Author of Life by rebelling against him, they opened the door to sickness, suffering, and death. Much like the patient who walked out of an oxygen tent only to find he couldn't breathe, so our first parents "walked out" on their source of life, and had to live with the consequences of their free choice. The third and arguably the most devastating effect of this original sin was that all their descendants would be born into this world lacking the grace that had been available to Adam and Eve, and for which we had been made.

Say, for example, your grandmother wins the lottery tomorrow. While you are anxiously awaiting to find out how much your percentage will be as your inheritance, your grandma is at the race track with the money trying to double it. Assuming she loses everything, you would be in the same state we are all in now in relation to God. Our first parents did "blow" our inheritance, something that was not really ours in the first place. Thus, being born with original sin really means that you lack the supernatural graces or "inheritance" God had intended for you to have. The doctrine of original sin does not mean that all babies have some kind of positive sin on their souls for which they are responsible.

The sin of our first parents also upset the order of creation established by God. If we imagine the order of creation as a two pan scale, the rebellion of mere creatures against the Creator threw the scale permanently out of balance, thus making it impossible for any of those same creatures to relate to God in the same way ever again. No action by any finite creature could have adequately fixed the scale. God could have left us in that situation or could have even destroyed all of creation. But as we will see so often, that is not the way our infinitely compassionate God operates.

Another more visual explanation might help illustrate this basic point. Suppose that in the beginning, mankind enjoyed God's presence and lived with Him on top of a mountain. Their free sin of prideful disobedience fractured the mountain, so that now all mankind is separated from the mountain of God by a wide abyss. No matter how hard one of us tries, there is no way back to the mountain of God. God Himself must initiate the contact, which He did in the Person of Jesus Christ, who literally laid down His life for us and acts as a "bridge" over which we may cross over and enter full communion with God.

Immediately after the fall from grace of our first parents, we already see God promising to send a Savior to rescue mankind from its predicament (see Gen. 3:15). The Church teaches that not only did Jesus Christ the Savior restore the balance of the order of creation, but actually gave us an opportunity to live in an even higher state than that of Adam and Eve if we but share in His sufferings. As always, God brings a greater good out of what was apparently totally evil.

EXERCISE #7: Answer the following reflection questions in your journal: 1) List ten things for which you can be grateful to God. 2) In the light of this story of the creation and fall of mankind, what do you think is the meaning or purpose of your life?

CHAPTER SEVEN

BELIEVING IN JESUS CHRIST

The second article of the Apostles' Creed sums up God's response to the fall of mankind, in that it speaks of the identity of the One who was sent to save us from sin – Jesus Christ.

The name **"Jesus"** comes from the Hebrew name "Yeshua," which means "Yahweh is salvation" or "God saves." We see this name being revealed to both Mary (see Luke 1:30–31) and Joseph (see Mt. 1:20–21) by angelic messengers of God. Since it is the name of our Savior (cf. Acts 4:12), it should be used with respect and reverence, and never carelessly or in vain. In fact, it is a common custom (especially when praying) in the Church to bow one's head slightly when saying this name out of respect for the One who it represents.

The fact that Jesus is our *Savior* cannot be overemphasized. As we saw in the preceding chapter, the effects of the first sin of prideful disobedience by the first human beings were enormous. Mankind was left critically injured, with no hope of recovery. Our merciful and loving God did not leave us in this condition, but actually became one of us, when the Word of God, the Second Person of the Holy Trinity, became man. To rebalance the scales of the objective order, and to "redeem" or "save" mankind from its predicament, there needed to be a perfect and limitless act of *obedience* given by one with a human nature. Since no mere human being could offer such an act, Jesus Christ, the Son of God made man, offered such an act by His life, which culminated in His loving act of selflessness on the cross (see Rom. 5:19).

The word **"Christ"** comes from the Greek work "Christos," meaning "anointed one." "Christos" is the translation of the Hebrew word

"Mashiah," which also means "the anointed one." This Hebrew word is the source for the English word "Messiah." Thus, the words "Christ" and "Messiah" mean the same thing.

The words "Jesus" and "Christ" have been linked since the early Church, since "the Savior" was to be the "anointed one" of God (see Psalms 2:2; Luke 4:16–21). This anointing was a sign of being given special powers by God, and included a three–fold ministry. First, the anointed one was to be a prophet who revealed the will of God. Second, he was also to be a priest who helped his people to be holy by sacrificing on their behalf. Third, he was to be a good king who not only cared for His people, but served them as well. By His life, death, and resurrection, Jesus fulfilled all three of these ministries.

When we say Jesus is **"the only Son"** of God, we are not implying that we are not children of God (see Rom. 8:14–17). It simply means that Jesus Christ is the Son of God in a way no one else could ever be. He is, as the Nicene Creed states so well, "eternally begotten of the Father, God from God, light from light, true God from true God. Begotten, not made, one in being with the Father, through Him all things were made."

These very careful statements were the fruit of a tremendous struggle at the Council of Nicea in 325. At that time in the Church, many people had fallen into the error (called a "heresy") of believing that Jesus was not truly God. Led by a priest named Arius, the **Arian heresy** became very powerful and its influence was widespread. Through the working of the Holy Spirit at the Council of Nicea, however, their doctrine was soundly rejected. The lines quoted above from the Nicene Creed very clearly state that Jesus is truly divine, and is the Word of God, the Second Person of the Holy Trinity, **"Our Lord"** who rules the Universe, through whom all things were made (see John 1:1–4, 14).

EXERCISE #8: Answer the following reflection question in your journal and be ready to discuss it in class: Why was it so important for the Council of Nicea to affirm the divinity of Jesus Christ?

CHAPTER EIGHT

THE BLESSED MOTHER

Just as the second article of the creed preserves the *divinity* of Christ, so the third article of the Apostles' Creed preserves the *humanity* of Christ.

If Jesus is not really true God and true man, then there is no redemption, no salvation, no "rebalancing of the scales," and no "bridge" that stretches across the abyss that separates mankind from God. If Jesus is only God and not man, then our human nature still suffers the effects of the sin by our first parents, and we are still left without a real model for our human existence. If Jesus is only man and not God, there is absolutely no reason why we should listen to Jesus anymore than any other person. Further, there would be nothing unique or holy about the Church He established, and no reason whatever for promising to obey, support, or believe it.

Thus, we can see the Church has not engaged in idle debates over unimportant phrases. A small error in a word about the identity of Christ could have huge ramifications in the long run. Thus, the Church has defined that Jesus is One Divine Person with two natures: human and divine. Sadly, there have always been those who err by denying one half of this truth. In the last chapter we discussed the Arian heresy, which denied Jesus' divinity. In this chapter we will deal with people who denied Jesus' humanity. As early as the time of St. John the Apostle, some were beginning to doubt this important truth (cf. 2 John 7–11). Those who believed Jesus only "seemed" to be human were eventually called **"Docetists"**, (from the Greek verb "to seem").

We say in this third article of the Creed that Jesus was **"conceived by the Holy Spirit"**. God the Father, working through the Holy Spirit, "conceived" the Son of God in the womb of the virgin Mary. Though the Son of God has existed from all eternity along with the Father and the Holy Spirit, His human body was only fashioned inside His mother's womb several months before He was born. The feast of the Annunciation (March 25) celebrates the day the archangel Gabriel announced the coming birth of Jesus to Mary. The feast of the Incarnation, which we celebrate on Christmas, is the great celebration of the mystery that God became man to save us.

The Blessed Mother is noted in a special way with the words **"born of the Virgin Mary"** for two main reasons. The first reason is because authentic teaching about her invariably preserves authentic teaching about Jesus. When the Council of Ephesus in 431 declared Mary to be "Theotokos" or "Mother of God," it reiterated two important truths about Christ. First, since He had a mother, He must have really been human. Second, since she is the Mother of God, we may safely conclude that Jesus is God Himself.

The other main reason why Catholics place so much importance on Mary is because *God* did. Incredible as it may seem, God freely chose this teenage girl who would, by her free obedience, help Him redeem the world. The Fathers of Vatican II wrote very clearly about the unique role of Mary in their Dogmatic Constitution on the Church: "(J)ust as a woman had a share in bringing about death, so also a woman should contribute to life... the Fathers [the theologians of the early Church] see Mary not merely as passively engaged by God, but as freely cooperating in the work of man's salvation through faith and obedience." The document then quotes the second century bishop St. Irenaeus, who wrote that "the knot of Eve's disobedience was untied by Mary's obedience: what the virgin Eve bound through her disbelief, Mary loosened by her faith" (*Lumen Gentium*, #56). A few paragraphs later, the Fathers of the Council go on to say that "in a wholly singular way she cooperated by her obedience, faith, hope and burning charity in the work of the Savior in restoring supernatural life to souls. For this reason she is a mother to us in the order of grace" (*LG*, #61).

The Catholic Church has consistently handed on three main Marian beliefs through the ages. First, we believe that Mary was **immaculately conceived**. This does not mean Mary was conceived outside of the normal process for human procreation. It means that in anticipation of the merits of Christ, God the Father (who is not limited by the bounds of human time) kept Mary free from original sin. In other words, because of her very special mission, God did not allow her to inherit that lack of grace that had plagued all mankind since the sin of the first human pair. It does not follow that Mary was "programmed" like a computer without free will. While she was indeed "full of grace" (see Luke 1:28), she was also just as free as Eve was to reject God. We are eternally in Mary's debt for her saying "yes" to God's invitation offered through the archangel Gabriel (see Luke 1:38).

A second important belief about Mary is that she was a **perpetual virgin**. Prophesied in the Old Testament (see Isaiah 7:14) and fulfilled in the New Testament (see Matthew 1:23), the Virgin Birth showed very clearly that *God* is the One who saves us. The fact that Mary remained a virgin after the birth of Jesus was consistently defended by such Fathers of the Early Church as St. Ambrose (339–397), Pope St. Leo I (5th century), and St. Augustine (354–430), and defined at the Second Council of Constantinople in A.D. 553.

The third major Marian doctrine is that at the end of her earthly life, she was **assumed body and soul into heaven** and currently enjoys what all of us will one day hopefully share with her. Pope Pius XII, after consultation with all the bishops of the world, solemnly defined this doctrine on November 1, 1950. These Marian doctrines preserve astonishingly good news for Christians. It means that "one of our own" has so freely and fully cooperated with God's grace that she has become for us a real mother, who cares for us *personally* and who prays for our salvation *individually*! Everyone in the Church is encouraged to honor her, speak with her in prayer, and imitate her life of virtue in whatever state of life we find ourselves.

EXERCISE #9: Answer the following reflection question in your journal and be ready to discuss it in class: If you had fifteen minutes to spend with Blessed Virgin Mary, what would you want to talk about? Prepare a list of ten questions.

CHAPTER NINE

NO GREATER LOVE

The fourth article of the Creed focuses on the redemptive Passion of Jesus Christ; that is, the fact that he **"suffered under Pontius Pilate, was crucified, and died";** in other words, the suffering that Our Lord endured so that we might be redeemed.

Jesus, because He shared our human nature, shrank from pain just as we do (see Luke 22:42–43). He chose to patiently endure it out of love for us rather than reject it, though, which He could have easily done (see Matthew 26:52–54). The Church teaches that Jesus suffered inconceivable spiritual, emotional, and physical pain. First and foremost, His spiritual sufferings included some kind of mystical vision of all the sins of mankind, since it was for all of those that He was dying. He also suffered the emotional pain of rejection and humiliation as well as the physical pains associated with Roman torture. Pontius Pilate, the Roman governor of Judea at the time, was the one who ordered his "scourging" and execution.

As the Scripture accounts show, Jesus, the Word of God Incarnate totally free of all sin, was mercilessly whipped by Roman soldiers. The whips commonly used for this purpose were long leather strips with bits of bone tied to the ends. It was quite possible for a victim of this scourging to suffer several broken ribs and even die right then and there. Even after a "crown" of piercing thorns was jammed onto His head, however, Jesus was still able to carry a heavy wooden crossbeam up and out of the city limits to the permanent racks the Romans had set up for their crucifixions along one of the public roads entering Jerusalem. Stripped and shivering, nails were then driven through His wrists and feet, and He was hoisted upon the scaffolding.

Crucified people died slowly, since their hanging body weight made it gradually more and more difficult to breathe. Many hours later, after extreme anguish, the person would die of suffocation. Sometimes, in order to hasten death, the soldiers would break the legs of the prisoners so that they would not be able to push up on the cross with their feet in an attempt to get more air. Jesus had already died by the time they came round to do this, however, but a soldier stabbed Him through the heart with the point of his lance (see John 19:34) to make sure Jesus was dead.

Incredible as it might seem, Jesus freely chose this most gruesome way to die to show us that His love has no limits. He could have accomplished the Redemption in some other manner, but He took upon Himself the most unfair and cruel punishment so as to show the incredible love He has for each of us (Gal. 2:20).

Christ also died to give us an example of how we should live our lives. Christ certainly does not want all of us to *literally* imitate Him by volunteering to be crucified by civil authorities. He does, however, want us to imitate the *charity* (see John 15:13), *humility* (see Phil. 2:6–8), *obedience* (see Romans 5:19), and *patience* (see Isaiah 53:7) which He so perfectly showed us by hanging on a cross.

Many people today still wonder, though, why Jesus had to die. "Couldn't He have shown us His love and given us an example of how to live without having to die so terribly?" For the answer to this question, we must go back to the fall of mankind we discussed in chapter six. The sin of prideful disobedience by our first parents upset the objective order of creation God had established. This order could only be set aright by the *humble obedience* of the God–Man Jesus Christ. This is why St. Paul writes in his Epistle to the Romans that "just as through the disobedience of one man the many were made sinners, so through the obedience of one man the many will be made righteous" (Romans 5:19). Jesus freely took on the punishment of sin (death, pain, and suffering) even though He did not deserve any of it, to save sinners from this same punishment and give them the opportunity of living forever with Him in heaven. Never before or since has the world seen such infinitely powerful love. "Love is made perfect through suffering" (cf. Heb. 2:10).

Lastly, this article speaks of Jesus being **"buried"**. The Gospel writers described in great detail the death and burial of Our Lord so as to leave no doubt about the truthfulness of the Resurrection (see Mark 15:37–47 and John 19:31–42). It is very interesting to note that a thirteen and a half by four and a quarter feet shroud in which Jesus was reportedly buried is reported to have been preserved and is now on display at the Cathedral of Turin, Italy. The burial cloth bears an image (much like a photo negative) of a man approximately 5"11" tall who had been tortured and crucified naked. Fr. Francis Filas, a Jesuit priest and professor of theology at Loyola University in Chicago well versed in information about the "Holy Shroud of Turin," notes that over one of the eyes of the man on the shroud there exist six Greek letters from a Roman coin that was minted only during the years of the reign of Pontius Pilate and only in Palestine. It was common practice back then to place a coin on the eyes of a dead person to keep their eyes shut. Although many scholars have testified as to its authenticity, the Church has not yet officially ruled on the validity of this apparent relic.

EXERCISE #10: Answer the following reflection question in your journal: Whom do you know would die for you? Whom would you die for?

CHAPTER TEN

THE PASCHAL MYSTERY

The Resurrection of Jesus Christ is the most important event yet in recorded human history as far as Christians are concerned, and is the subject of our next article of the Apostles' Creed.

By the time of Christ, most Jews believed in a place or state where the souls of the just went after death. Referred to as "the hell of the just," "the abode of the dead," or "the limbo of the fathers," this is the place where the Church teaches the soul of Christ descended after His death on the cross, while His body remained in the tomb. Jesus **"descended into hell"** for two main reasons.

First, He desired to take on the full effect of sin. God did not design the beautiful and mysterious unity of body and soul that constitute a human being to be separated. This was one of the tragic results of original sin, which Jesus Himself experienced so as to free us from its grip. Just as a mother may take a taste of medicine to show her child that there is nothing to be afraid of, so Our Lord tasted death in order to reassure His followers that everything will be all right if we but trust in Him. A second reason Jesus descended to the dead was to reassure the spirits of those who had gathered there that their time of deliverance was at hand. No one, no matter how "good," had a right to enter God's presence until Christ's selfless obedience made the redemption of human beings possible. As the *Catechism* teaches, "Jesus did not descend into hell to deliver the damned, nor to destroy the hell of damnation, but to free the just who had gone before him" (CCC, #633).

The creed next states that **"on the third day he rose again"**. This must be understood in the Jewish sense of time, and not ours. For the Jews, any part of a day counted as a full day. Thus, even though Jesus spent somewhere around 40 hours in the tomb, they still referred to it as three days.

In any case, the Resurrection of Jesus represents the reunification of Jesus' now glorified body with His soul. His resurrection is fundamentally different than that of Lazarus, the widow's son, Jairus' daughter, etc., since Jesus was raised to a supernatural level of existence, while the people He had cured were only brought back to this natural life. His Resurrection was the crowning miracle that showed conclusively both His divinity and authority, and completed what is known as the "**Paschal Mystery;**" that is, His "Passover" from death to life. By rising from the dead He proved He conquered sin and showed us the promise of eternal life (see Luke 24:1–49).

St. Paul notes in his letter to the Corinthians that the Resurrection is absolutely central to Christianity: "If Christ has not been raised, then empty [too] is our preaching; empty, too, your faith... If for this life only we have hoped in Christ, we are the most pitiable people of all" (see 1 Corinthians 15:12–19).

EXERCISE #11: Answer the following reflection questions in your journal and be prepared to discuss them in class: 1) How can you, as Christ did when He descended to the dead, show concern and compassion for people who have died? 2) Where could you go today if you wanted to experience the Resurrected Jesus?

*"When the Son of Man comes in his glory,
and all the angels with him,
he will sit upon his glorious throne"* (Matthew 24:31).

CHAPTER ELEVEN

CHRIST WILL COME AGAIN

The sixth article of the Creed tells us Jesus **"ascended into heaven"**, an event which, according to the book of *Acts* (see Acts 1:9–11), took place 40 days after Easter. At this point, and after apparently a number of post–Easter appearances, Our Lord's earthly mission finally ended and He entered His glory. As St. Paul mentions in his letter to the Colossians, Jesus' ascension can remind us to keep our hopes and focus on heaven, and not just here on the earth (see Col. 3:1–2).

When we next say that Jesus **"is seated at the right hand of the Father"**, we are speaking metaphorically. Since God is pure spirit, the Father has no physical hand. Nor is there a "throne" somewhere in the skies upon which Christ sits. This phrase is a symbolic one that really means Jesus is equal to God and shares in the Father's power and authority (see Mark 14:62; Ps. 110:1).

Immediately after this article, we see the promise of Christ to **"come again to judge the living and the dead"**. Though no one knows the day nor the hour (see Acts 1:7), and whether we are ready or not, Jesus has promised to return to earth (see Mt. 24:29–31; Luke 17:22–37; et. al.).

The seventh article of the Apostles' Creed speaks about how Christ will judge us. Scripture is quite clear that at the end of our earthly lives, Jesus Christ will evaluate us on how well we have responded to His invitation (see Acts 10:42; Hebrews. 9:27; et. al.). Our Lord repeated many times that only those who actually *do* the will of God will be saved (see Mt. 7:21; et. al.). This just makes sense, since actions speak louder than words. Imagine a boyfriend is found to be constantly "cheating" on his girlfriend. Yet every week he goes out with his original girlfriend, never apologizing (since he doesn't believe what he did was wrong) but all the while claiming he "loves" her. How long do you think it will take before

43

the girl catches on to his hypocrisy and drops him like a hot potato? In the same way, we cannot simply claim to love God and yet at the same time do things He detests and still expect to live with Him forever in peace and joy.

The Church has taught there are two kinds of judgment. The **Particular judgment** refers to that judgment which will occur when individuals, at the moment of death, will be judged immediately by Christ. The **General Judgment** is the judgment given by Christ at the end of the world. Let us now examine both of these in more detail. This should hopefully be of very great interest to us, since every day we are moving closer to both!

As have discussed earlier, the body and soul of a person separate at the moment of death. While the body remains on earth and, generally speaking, begins to decay, the soul is brought to Christ, whereupon the person is sent to hell, heaven, or purgatory (see Luke 16:19–31). Since we will be looking at the concepts of heaven and hell a bit later, we will now limit our discussion to the last place mentioned, purgatory.

Purgatory is a temporary state of cleansing for those souls on their way to heaven. We know from Scripture that nothing unclean can enter heaven (see Rev. 21:27). It stands to reason, then, that people who die in a state of grace yet still have unforgiven venial sins on their souls or who have not yet sufficiently made up for the temporal effects of their already forgiven sins need to undergo some kind of "cleansing" or "purging" before they will admitted into God's presence (see Mt. 12:32, 36–37; 1 Corinthians. 3:10–15). The punishment in purgatory is primarily a tremendous pain of loss, in that the souls there know it is only through their own fault that they have been delayed from enjoying the "**Beatific Vision**;" that is, living in God's presence and "seeing Him face to face." While in purgatory the souls will also become aware of all the missed opportunities they had to show love or make up for sin that were lost because of foolishness, selfishness, or ignorance, which will add to the pain experienced there. Yet, since these souls also will be filled with the certain hope of heaven, their pain will be seen as part of a healing process by which they will be made more healthy and better able to share in the awesome love of God.

Purgatory is not a place where people get "one more chance" to live a good life, nor is it a place that lasts forever. Purgatory will no longer exist after the General Judgment, when "all the nations" will be judged and the earth shall pass away (see Mt. 25:31–46). The General Judgment is also referred to as "the Day of the Lord" in the Old Testament (see Is. 2:11–12; Joel 2:1–2), and it is entirely possible that some people will be living on the earth upon Christ's return (see Luke 18:8).

Reflecting on this article of the Creed should promote in us a healthy fear of judgment. Just as a healthy fear of prison keeps many people from committing certain crimes, so should our healthy fear of eternal punishment keep us from committing certain sins. Of course, the best motive for avoiding sin is not simply a fear of punishment, but because of a great love for God and a strong desire to live with Him forever in heaven.

We should also consider taking advantage of the present time of mercy we now enjoy. Every moment of every day is a tremendous gift from our loving God to help us get closer to Him. Once we die, however, we cannot do any more. Our lives are like clay that can be worked freely right up until the minute it is put into the kiln, whereupon it hardens and cannot be molded any longer. Perhaps we could prepare for our upcoming "Interview" with the all–merciful Lord Jesus by practicing good works and performing acts of repentance (see 1 Peter 4:8).

EXERCISE #12: Answer the following reflection questions in your journal and be prepared to discuss them in class: 1) List five specific acts, no matter how small, you could do within the next 24 hours that could help prepare you for the coming judgment. 2) What would you do if you knew you only had six months to live?

CHAPTER TWELVE

THE HOLY SPIRIT

As we discussed the second article of the creed in chapter seven, we saw that the Council of Nicea elaborated on the Church's understanding of Christ, the Second Person of the Holy Trinity. In a similar way, the First Council of Constantinople in 381 clarified the teaching on the Third Person of the Holy Trinity, the Holy Spirit. Its teaching became part of what has been passed down to us as the Nicene Creed.

We believe **"the Holy Spirit"** is "the Lord"; that is, He is not a created or a dependent being, but the Third Person of the Holy Trinity, God Himself. The Spirit is "the Giver of Life," since it is only through the Spirit of God that anything has life (see Gen. 2:7). When we say that the Holy Spirit "proceeds from the Father and the Son," we mean that there is an eternal exchange of love between the Three Persons of the Holy Trinity, that heavenly society from which all human societies (especially the family) have their origin and source. The Holy Spirit is to be "worshiped and glorified" with the Father and the Son, since He is not just some "thing" but some*one*: He is a Divine Person, the very Love of God, worthy of our adoration (see John 4:23). The phrase "He has spoken through the prophets" validates the Old Testament, much like the Transfiguration of Christ did on Mt. Tabor (see Mt. 17:1–8).

The Holy Spirit is the life of the Church, the "soul" of the Body of Christ on earth. The Spirit of God guides the Church of Christ into all Truth (see John 14:26; 16:13), protecting it from teaching error in matters of faith and morals so that "the gates of the netherworld shall not prevail against it" (Mt. 16:18). The Holy Spirit also grants to the Church certain "charismatic" gifts for the good of all the faithful (see 1 Corinthians 12:1–11).

The Holy Spirit comes to dwell within each one of us when we are baptized and confirmed (see Eph. 4:30). It is this Spirit living in us that transforms our lives, granting to us seven "sanctifying" gifts (see Isaiah 11:2–3) which make us holier and better servants of Our Lord. **Wisdom** helps us to truly know God's will for our lives, and **understanding** enables us to appropriate our faith by "making it our own" so that we can spread it more effectively. It is through the gift of **knowledge** that we can come to have a better relationship with the Lord; that is, to truly "know" Him in a personal way. The gift of **fortitude** helps us to be courageous in our defense of the Faith, whereas the gift of **counsel** aids us in making right judgments, which are essential to the living of a good moral life (see Ezekiel 36:26–27). **Piety** means that we will made more prayerful, reverent, and holy. **Fear of the Lord** does not mean being afraid of going to Church! It means having a holy and healthy fear of God Almighty, the One who created the universe, who alone deserves our adoration in awe and wonder.

EXERCISE #13: Answer the following reflection question in your journal: **Which gift of the Holy Spirit do you think you could use the most right now in your life?**

CHAPTER THIRTEEN

THE FAMILY OF GOD

This chapter will cover the two related subjects covered together in the ninth article of the creed—**"the holy catholic Church"** and **"the communion of saints"**. It makes a great deal of sense for the article describing the Church to follow immediately after the section of the creed concerning the Holy Spirit, for it was through the Spirit of God that the Catholic Church was born on Pentecost (see Acts 2:1–13). Nearly two millennia later, the same Holy Spirit is even now the source of the life and vitality of the same Catholic Church.

The Church is much more than an optional social club for people who happen to say they believe in Jesus. It is the very Body of Christ, to which we are joined in baptism and by which we pass from death in sin to new life in Christ. Ever since the early Church, Christians have understood the communal nature of full life in Christ (see Acts 2:42–47; 4:32–37). The Church has taught that Jesus Himself founded the Church upon Peter, "the rock" (see Mt. 16:18), and has pointed through the ages to the abundant testimony given in the letters of St. Paul. Not only does Paul present the Church as a social reality, but also as *the means by which* we are saved in Christ (see Rom. 6:4–5; Eph. 2:19–22; Col. 1:18).

The Church has been described as the "extension of Christ's presence throughout history." Just as Jesus Christ fulfilled His role as the anointed one by being a prophet, priest, and king, so His Church continues this threefold ministry throughout the ages. By teaching the faithful the truths our Lord taught, the Church continues His prophetic role. By helping to make Her members holy and by perpetuating the sacrifice of Christ on Calvary by way of the Mass, the Church continues Jesus' priestly ministry. Lastly, by ruling the faithful in Christ's name, the Church continues His ministry as king.

Furthermore, the Nicene Creed summarized four "marks" or characteristics that the Church of Jesus Christ would have. First, the Church should be **one** in that it be united in belief and worship and under a single head (see John 10:16). Second, the Church must be **holy** in that it aims to help make and keep her members holy ("saints"), and, despite certain scandals, should give a model of holiness to the world (see Mt. 5:16). Third, Christ's Church should be truly "**catholic**" or universal; that is, present to all people of all times in all places (see Mt. 28:19). Fourth, the Church should be **apostolic**. The true Church should be able to trace its teachings and authority back to the apostles, and hence to Christ (see Luke 10:16).

The Catholic Church has always taught that it alone is the only church which fulfills all these requirements, though many others can share in these marks. The Catholic Church is **one** in that it is the pope who keeps order within the household of God. While some popes are more successful at this than others, there always exists in the Church an ultimate authority that can be trusted to at least not teach error (see chapter five). The Church is **holy** in that it has presented through the ages and continues to present today thousands of personal models of holiness in the form of formally recognized ("canonized") saints. There are also the millions of saints known only to God who took advantage of the tremendous treasury of graces Mother Church offers and "worked out their salvation" (see Phil. 2:12) under her care.

In spite of all this, it is a sad and unavoidable fact of human history that not everyone in the family of God performs as well as he or she ought. Jesus Himself warned that His followers would sometimes disgrace Him and would even cause great harm among the family of God (see Mt. 13:24–30; 18:6–7). Even so, this does not disprove that the Catholic Church is the true Church. It does prove, however, one of the main messages the Church has to offer the world; namely, that all of us are sinners in need of God's mercy.

The Catholic Church also fulfills the requirement of being **catholic** or universal, since it has indeed been open to people of all races, places, times, and social standing. The universal church must be truly that to adequately reflect the incredible love God has for each and every one of His creatures. Finally, the Church is also apostolic, since it can trace not only its tradition of episcopal ordinations and authority back to the apostles, but its moral and doctrinal teachings as well. John Henry Newman, a brilliant scholar and professor at Oxford in the 19th century, converted from Anglicanism to Catholicism after his study of the early Church convinced him that the Catholic religion really was the only truly apostolic communion among all the various Christian religions.

Here is what Pope Paul VI and the bishops of the Second Vatican Council taught about this matter:

> The one mediator, Christ, established and ever sustains here on earth his holy Church, the community of faith, hope, and charity, as a visible organization through which he communicates truth and grace to all men... This is the sole Church of Christ which in the Creed we profess to be one, holy, catholic, and apostolic, which our Saviour, after his resurrection, entrusted to Peter's pastoral care (Jn. 21:17), commissioning him and the other apostles to extend and rule it (see Mt. 28:18, etc.), and which he raised up for all ages as "the pillar and mainstay of the truth" (1 Tim. 3:15). This Church, constituted and organized as a society in the present world, subsists in the Catholic Church, which is governed by the successor of Peter and by the bishops in communion with him. Nevertheless, many elements of sanctification and of truth are found outside of her visible confines. Since these are gifts belonging to the Church of Christ, they are forces impelling towards Catholic unity (*Lumen Gentium*, #8).

This does not mean in any way that all Catholics necessarily go to heaven and all non– Catholics necessarily go to hell. Rather, the Church teaches that only those who truly know that the Catholic church is the ordinary means by which God has chosen to continue His work on earth and who *then* stubbornly refuse to join have shut themselves out of eternal joy. As a matter of fact, Catholics are taught that they will be judged more severely because they have been given more.

The Church has faithfully handed down the "Deposit of Faith" Christ gave to His Apostles, with all the aids to salvation and happiness that includes, (e.g., the sacraments, teaching authority, etc.). The Catholic Church is the *ordinary means* of salvation Christ has established for the salvation of the world. While it is certainly possible for some people to work out their salvation outside the ordinary means, it is important to remember that Christ *wants* us to use these ordinary means, and even gave His life, out of love, so that we might have access to them!

EXERCISE #14: Answer the following reflection question in your journal and be prepared discuss your answer in class: List five serious differences in doctrine or moral teachings that exist between the Catholic Church and one other religious group (e.g., Protestant Christianity, Judaism, Buddhism, etc.).

Now we come to the second part of the ninth article of the Creed, where we will explore Catholic teaching on the saints. The Church teaches that the saints are people who have died who have been rewarded for their faith and love and who now experience life with God in heaven.

Catholics pay special honor to the saints for several reasons. First of all, it is quite natural for human beings to have heroes. One glance up and down a high school hallway shows hundreds of pictures of famous celebrities posted inside lockers. These "heroes" reveal something about the person who admires them. If a student next to you had pictures of mass murderers, rapists, and evil dictators pasted on their locker door, you would certainly look at them differently than if they had pictures of their puppies and teddy bear collection.

In the same way, it is very natural to have heroes in the religious life. If we admire the strength and perseverance of a professional athlete who consistently performs well under adversity, why can't we admire the strength and perseverance of a Mother Teresa, an elderly woman who has pulled thousands of poor and sick homeless people from the streets of Calcutta?

The Church has consistently taught that it is a good practice to honor the saints, though cautioning against worshiping them in place of God. The Second Vatican Council's *Lumen Gentium* (#50) explained

> It is supremely fitting, therefore, that we love those friends and fellow heirs of Jesus Christ, who are also our brothers and extraordinary benefactors, that we render due thanks to God for them and "suppliantly invoke them and have recourse to their prayers, their power and help in obtaining benefits from God through His Son, Jesus Christ, our Lord, who is our sole Redeemer and Savior." For by its very nature every genuine testimony of love which we show to those in heaven tends toward and terminates in Christ, who is the "crown of all saints." Through Him it tends toward and terminates in God, who is wonderful in His saints and is magnified in them.

One may rightly ask at this point: "Why does God bother with saints? Why can't people come directly to Him?" The answer can be found by looking at the whole process by which God has chosen to redeem us. As we noted earlier in chapter six, God has given mankind a staggering amount of freedom and responsibility. Even though our first parents misused these great gifts, God still trusts us with them, even asking that we put them into His service by *cooperating* with Him as He redeems the world. We mentioned in chapter eight that the Virgin Mary was asked by God to "untie the knot" of Eve's disobedience. When God set up the way we are redeemed, He included an element of human participation in that redemption. It is in this way that we can work out our own salvation by helping others get to heaven at the same time.

The saints are people who lived this lesson to the fullest. They "magnified" the Lord in that those who saw their lives saw the Love of God more clearly. They became holy, despite their sins, by serving God through serving other people in faith, hope, and charity. This service to others does not only not stop with their bodily deaths, but actually increases and extends to all the faithful in the Church when they are called back "home." In this way the saints act as "intercessors" or mediators of God's favor on our behalf.

With this in mind, then, we can better understand the traditional designation of three groups within the Church, the Mystical Body of Christ which transcends time and space. First, there is the **Church Militant**, those members of the Church on earth struggling to bring God to the world. Next, there is the **Church Suffering**, those members of the Church who are being purged or purified of their sins in Purgatory. Last, there is the **Church Triumphant**, those members of the Church who are now in glory with God in heaven. Since all the members of these different groups still belong to the same Body, we can lean on each other for support and help one another as needed. The Church Triumphant is obviously not in need of help, but can aid both of the other groups. The Church Suffering and the Church Militant can receive help from each other or from the Church Triumphant and can offer help to one another. This is all part of God's glorious plan of redemption.

For these reasons, Catholics believe it is very healthy to pray to the saints, asking them for help and guidance. This, too, is a very natural thing for human beings to do. We are always turning to friends and family for assistance with problems that come up in our everyday lives. Similarly, praying to the saints is simply asking our "big brothers and sisters" within the family of God to aid us in some way.

This time honored practice of the Catholic Church is also well substantiated in Scripture. On several occasions, St. Paul specifically asks for the prayers of his people (see Rom. 15:30; Eph. 6:18–19; et. al.). In Revelation 5:8, we see the prayers of the saints being brought before God. Also, in John 2:1–11, Jesus performs His first public miracle at the request of His mother.

These are again examples of how God wants us to ask for things and to lean on each other for support so that we can learn the ways of the Love that is lived perfectly in heaven.

Some may wonder about times people pray to the saints for a certain favor and are refused. We must first keep in mind that God has promised us He answers all prayers. Sometimes He answers in ways we do not expect or in ways we cannot see, but He does indeed hear all prayers. Secondly, we should remember that it is very possible for us to ask wrongly. A prayer that your English teacher catches pneumonia the morning your term paper is due might not be answered affirmatively by our loving God! Third, we should be aware that God's grace builds on nature. In other words, sometimes God wants us to show that we are doing our share before He gives us something. Some people could, conceivably, sit around eating doughnuts and watching reruns of old cartoons all day, praying to God that He send them $50,000 a year. But it would certainly not be in their best long–term interest if God answered their prayer in the way they wanted. Finally, saints can never do anything that is against the will of God, so it is useless to try to play off a saint against God. Despite the times our prayers to or through the saints seem to go unanswered, we should always recall that prayer to the saints is an incredibly powerful tool given to us by the infinitely loving Lord of all creation.

Another sign of Catholic devotion to the saints is the use of statues, pictures, relics, etc. of the saints. Some fundamentalists condemn this practice as idolatrous, citing the command in Exodus 20:4 to not carve any images of created things. Such a strict interpretation of this passage is inaccurate; it would also lead to the destruction of all family photographs, locks of hair, and baby dolls. There really is no need to fear Catholics are violating this Commandment, because Scripture shows that certain images or relics, when used in accord with God's plan, can actually be helpful (see Num. 21:6–9; Mt. 14:36; Acts 19:12). Lastly, several inspired Church councils [e.g., Nicea II (787), Vatican I (1870), et. al.] have not only permitted but actually *recommended* the use of images, statues, relics, and other devotional items by the faithful.

EXERCISE #15: Answer the following reflection questions in your journal and be prepared discuss your answers in class: 1) Who are your heroes and why? 2) Have you ever asked for something in prayer and later been glad it wasn't answered in the way you had first hoped? 3) Who is your patron saint?

CHAPTER FOURTEEN

LIFE EVERLASTING

This chapter will close our section on the Apostles' Creed, and consists of the last three articles. Each of them are very short, but all are extremely important and provide a "grand finale" to this rich treasure of belief we call the Apostles' Creed.

The tenth article on **"the forgiveness of sins"** follows right after the article that mentions the holy catholic Church, since it is through her that Jesus' saving work is continued. Throughout the Gospel accounts, we see Jesus constantly forgiving sins (see Mt. 9:1–8; Mk. 2:1–12; Luke 7:36–50; Jn. 8:3–11; et. al.). Though His whole life was meant to effect the forgiveness of sins, Jesus did institute the sacraments of Baptism and Penance that would extend this ministry of mercy throughout time. We see Our Lord giving special power and authority to the Apostles to forgive sins in His Name at several points in the Gospels (see Mt. 16:19, 18:18; Luke 24:46–47; John 20:22–23), and the Church has understood this is a commission from God Himself. The forgiveness of sins in the Name of Jesus is such an important part of Christianity that it has come down to us as one of the basic articles of the faith.

The next article speaks of **"the resurrection of the body"**. As we discussed in chapter ten, bodily death and the separation of our body and soul are the results of the sin of our first parents. Even though our bodies begin to rot and decay, our souls remain immortal (see Wisdom 3:1–4) and will be reunited with our "spiritual" or "heavenly" bodies (see 1 Corinthians 15:44, 49) at the end of time at the General Judgment to be taken either to hell or heaven (see John 5:28–29). We have a certain hope this will happen not only because of Christ's promise (see John 6:54; 11:17–27) but also because of the Assumption of Mary, who was given the special favor of receiving at the end of her earthly life what we all hope one day to receive at the General Judgment. Needless to say, the

Church's teaching on this subject clearly shows the wondrous dignity of the human body and why the idea of "reincarnation" is absolutely incompatible with Christianity (see Hebrews 9:27).

The last article speaks of the last things; namely, **"life everlasting"**. We know precious little of what exactly life will be like either in heaven or hell. We do know, however, that the joy that will be experienced in heaven from the "Beatific Vision" ("seeing God" or living in God's presence) is absolutely beyond our comprehension (see 1 Corinthians 2:9; Rev. 21:4). The physical and spiritual pain that will be experienced in hell is likewise beyond our comprehension at this point (see Mark 9:48; Isaiah 66:24), although we can say that the eternal separation from God would be the most terrible agony possible.

Perhaps this article was put last in the Creed so that we are reminded every time we pray it to put these truths into practice in our lives so that we may live uprightly and indeed reach heaven and avoid hell. The word **"Amen"** is Hebrew for "so be it!" This ends the prayer and represents our pledge to live it out.

EXERCISE #16: Answer the following reflection question in your journal and be prepared to discuss it in class: Think of a situation you have witnessed this past week in which two people hurt each other. How could the forgiveness of God bring healing to the situation?

CHAPTER FIFTEEN

GRACE AND SACRAMENTS

It is important never to forget that God, who made us out of nothing and who loves each one of us more than we can possibly imagine, never ceases to invite us to grow closer to Him by living the faith we profess in our daily lives. He gives us the ability to accomplish this difficult mission by bestowing grace on us through the seven sacraments. A thorough knowledge of these seven crucial instruments of God's loving plan is absolutely necessary when investigating the basics of the Catholic faith.

Grace can be defined, generally speaking, as supernatural power freely given to human beings by God (because of the merits of Jesus Christ) to help us get closer to Him. There are two types of grace. **Sanctifying grace** is that type of grace which can be described as a share of God's life in our souls (see 1 Corinthians 3:16–17). As we saw earlier in the first article of the Creed, our first parents enjoyed living in this state but sinned through pride, thus losing this precious gift. This "fall from grace" of our first parents was what caused sickness, pain, and death to enter the world, and threatened to separate mankind forever from its origin, purpose, and destiny in God. The effects of this "original sin" by the first man and woman have been felt by all their descendants, since every human being is now born into this world without the sanctifying grace we were supposed to have from birth.

Mankind would have remained in this wretched state were it not for Jesus' incredible saving act of selfless love on the Cross, through which we are given the power and strength to live out God's law and to once again become children of God (see Rom. 8:1–13). Christians first receive sanctifying grace at their baptism, and are expected to deepen this life of grace within them throughout their entire lives. Just how Christians "live out their baptism" will be explained in the chapters that follow.

Actual graces are more temporary influences from God that keep our minds on Him and direct our wills to doing what He wants (e.g., impulses to pray, reconcile with enemies, do a good deed, etc.). Though actual graces are showered upon every human being (not just Christians) constantly each day, people respond in different ways to them depending on their interior dispositions. Without the grace of God, we are totally powerless to live a holy life. Thus, remaining in a "state of grace," or staying in right relationship with the Lord, is extremely important. This is accomplished in part by the frequent and rightful reception of the sacraments which God Incarnate instituted for our benefit. The remaining part of this chapter deals with each of the seven sacraments individually.

Sacraments are defined in the *Catechism of the Catholic Church* as "efficacious signs of grace, instituted by Christ and entrusted to the Church, by which divine life is dispensed to us" (CCC, #1131). Let us examine this definition closely.

First of all, we speak of the sacraments as "signs." They are a unique kind of sign, though, because they actually *give* the grace they signify; they are "efficacious." They are visible signs of an invisible reality, and are the means God uses to confer blessings on us. Human beings need such simple signs for the following reasons. First, since we are not angels but human beings who depend upon the material world for information, simple signs like the ones used in the sacraments help us to understand what is actually occurring. Second, our limited human intellects might need some examples from common experience to help us understand Jesus' main points. Third, we need to be made ever more humble by submitting to a simple sign, whether that is water, oil, or bread (cf. 2 Kings 5:9–14). Lastly, by using simple signs that have been made or prepared by human hands, we are reminded once again of the beauty of God's plan of redemption and of how other human beings have been asked by God to help us get closer to Him.

It should be noted here that God's grace is not limited to the seven sacraments. God is not bound by His sacraments, and works in mysterious and wonderful ways far beyond the comprehension of human beings. Thus, it is very possible for someone outside the visible Church who has no access to the sacraments to receive grace and be saved. This does not mean, however, that the sacraments are unimportant or that Christians should never try to spread their faith. On the contrary, the sacraments are the divinely–ordained *ordinary* means of distributing God's grace on earth and sharing His love with the human family. They are so important Christ literally died to give us access to them (see John 19:34–35), and expressly commanded His disciples to carry them to the ends of the earth (see Matthew 28:19–20).

*"For to his angels he has
given command about you,
that they guard you in all
your ways"* (Psalm 91:11).

EXERCISE #17: Answer the following reflection question in your journal: Describe three times in your life where you knew you needed the special help and power of God.

The *Catechism* also claims that the sacraments are "instituted by Christ and entrusted to the Church." The Catholic Church teaches that Jesus Christ instituted and continues to sustain all seven sacraments. The Council of Trent in the 16th century taught that "the sacraments of the Catholic Church are seven in number, as is proved from Scripture, from the tradition handed down to us from the Fathers, and from the authority of the Councils" (Session 7, Canon 1). Furthermore, our Lord used simple material things (e.g., water, bread, wine, oil) because they were and are common to all societies, and so their significance (e.g., cleansing, nourishment, strength) would be better understood by all people.

Sacraments are the means by which God grants His grace to souls. Much like a prism refracts pure white light into seven distinct colors, so the sacraments are seven distinct yet intimately related channels of the light of God's love. Sacraments confer grace *ex opere operato*, which means "by the work worked" in Latin. In other words, the sacraments give grace not by virtue of the personal worthiness of the particular minister who is performing the rite, but by virtue of the sacrament itself. Thus, while obviously not ideal, a priest in serious sin or even certain kinds of heresy can validly perform the sacraments, even though by doing so he commits the serious sin of sacrilege. The real Minister of all the sacraments is Jesus Christ Himself, working through His ministers on earth. At a baptism, Jesus is baptizing; at an Anointing, Jesus is the One who heals; at a confession, Jesus forgives; and at the Eucharist, Jesus offers Himself.

Just how effectively the grace offered is actually received by the recipient of the sacrament, however, depends in part on the interior disposition (attitude, knowledge, moral state, et. al.) with which one receives a sacrament.

Sacraments are also the means by which we begin to participate in eternal life with God. They are the "doors" through which we may enter God's house. They bring people into God's family, nourish them with spiritual food, and help them remain faithful, happy, and focused on the Lord. They are the extension of Christ's power and presence throughout history, and are the means by which people today can encounter Christ in substantially the same way as people did in Palestine 2,000 years ago.

Though the sacraments may be divided into any number of different groups, we will begin our brief survey of these instruments of God's grace by focusing on the three sacraments of *initiation*; Baptism, Confirmation, and the Eucharist.

Baptism makes us members of the family of God by uniting us in a sacramental way with Christ Himself. Just as Christ was buried and was raised up to life everlasting, so those who are baptized and are faithful also look forward to the hope of heaven. Our "cleansing" is symbolized by the water that is poured over us or that into which we are immersed. Baptism is referred to as the first sacrament of initiation because it is through baptism that we are "born again" into God's family. Baptism is, as the *Catechism* says, "the basis of the whole Christian life, the gateway to life in the Spirit" (*CCC*, #1213).

The second sacrament of initiation, **Confirmation,** completes the sacrament of Baptism by making us fuller members of the Body of Christ. Through the power of this sacrament, the baptized are strengthened and made more capable of living out their witness to Christ in the modern world, and, "as true witness of Christ, more strictly obliged to spread and defend the faith by word and deed" (*CCC*, #1285).

The third sacrament of initiation is the **Eucharist**. The Blessed Sacrament is at the heart of the Church's sacramental life. All the sacraments really flow from and lead back into this Most Holy Sacrament, since It not just points to Christ, but *is* Christ. Christ longs to be with us every day and wants us to carry Him with us in our hearts as we go about our day. Thus, having sacrificed His life on the Cross for our salvation, Jesus gives us of His very self in Holy Communion, provided we are prepared to receive our King. Frequent and holy communions help strengthen our relationship with God, and make us more like Him.

There are two sacraments of *healing*: Penance and the Anointing of the Sick. **Penance**, also known as the sacrament of conversion, confession, or reconciliation, was called by many early Fathers of the Church a "second baptism"; for, by means of this sacrament, the baptized are cleansed of their sins committed after Baptism and reconciled to God. Christ established this sacrament on Easter Sunday night (see John 20:21–23) as a way of welcoming back into God's family those who were once thought to be lost. Regular reception of this sacrament, like Holy Communion, is an important help in living a virtuous life.

The **Anointing of the Sick** aims at strengthening both the bodies and the souls of the sick members of the Body of Christ. It helps those who are in danger of dying through some kind of illness or accident. Just as Jesus healed people in Palestine two thousand years ago, so He makes

His healing power available today through this sacrament. Regardless of whether or not the person regains his or her physical health, he or she has been strengthened by the grace of Christ through the power of the Holy Spirit to deal with the suffering and adversity that serious sickness involves.

The two sacraments of *vocation* are "at the service of communion," as the *Catechism* says, since they are directed towards the salvation of other people. **Holy Orders** is the sacrament that keeps the Church Herself living. Through the dedicated and selfless service of Her many bishops, priests, and deacons, the Church continues Jesus' ministry on earth: teaching, sanctifying, and ruling in His name. The ordained members of Christ's faithful people are to lay down their lives, as did Christ, in order to help their "flocks" stay close to the Good Shepherd.

Matrimony is the sacrament by which God's family on earth increases and multiplies. God himself is the author of marriage, and it is by means of this sacrament that two people grow in the grace and love of God and act as co–creators with God in the formation of a new family. Called to countless acts of selfless love each and every day in the home, married people take a long, sometimes difficult, but ultimately joyful path towards heaven. The grace of God helps couples to stay focused, selfless, and charitable. Many marriages that break up today are the unhappy result of a disregard for living in the grace of God.

EXERCISE #18: What do you remember about the sacraments you have received? What do you think your life would be like if you hadn't received any sacraments?

CHAPTER SIXTEEN

THE LIFE OF VIRTUE

The next main area of the Catholic Faith that we will study, as is outlined in the *Catechism of the Catholic Church*, is the "faith lived." We will look at the Ten Commandments and their place in your life as a young adult in today's modern world.

The reason God wants us to know and live by His moral law is because He loves us and wants us to be truly happy. He has bestowed on us a tremendous dignity by making us in His own image, with an intellect and a free will. Alone among all other bodily creatures, human beings have been found worthy to receive from God a law which holds the key to our freedom.

As we learned in chapter two when discussing the Argument from Conscience, there is no other source for the sense of objective morality all human beings possess other than God. Though some people try to get around this basic truth by claiming their sense of right and wrong comes from a "little voice," a "gut feeling," "what society says," or some vague notion of "whatever does not hurt others," all of these were shown to be inadequate in some way. This section will help you understand how we can know, with God's help, what is right from wrong. Since God made us and is sustaining our lives this very moment, we can confidently turn to Him for the answer to this very important question.

While it is certainly possible that God could trumpet down from the sky moral precepts every day at noon so that everyone in the world could hear Him, He obviously has not chosen to operate in this way. Rather, He has given us two sources of moral knowledge. The first is **human reason**, which gives us a certain, though imperfect, knowledge of that law which has been written on the hearts of all human beings. This is called the **"natural law"** since God made it a part of human nature (see Rom. 2:14–15). A good understanding of the natural law is basic to any healthy society, since it is on the basis of this law that all other laws are usually made. Hence, there are laws against murder, child abuse, stealing, perjury, bigamy (adultery), etc.

The other source of moral knowledge that God has given us is called **revelation**, since it contains what God has explicitly told us about Himself and what He expects of us. In the Old Testament, God's revelation of the Ten Commandments on Mt. Sinai reinforced and clarified the natural law. In the New Testament, God's perfect revelation in Jesus Christ fulfills what was given in the Old Testament. Our Lord simplified the law by summing it all up with His "law of love" (see Mt. 22:37–40). This is much more demanding, since now He has written it on our hearts (see Jeremiah 31:33). Now, we are judged not only by our outward conduct, but by our inward conduct as well (see Mt. 5). Thus, we can never be satisfied completely here on earth that we have lived this law out completely.

In other words, we are never finished carrying out Jesus' law of love. A parent would never say to a child, "Well, I've loved you full–time for six years now, I'm tired of it, so now you're on your own—good luck!" Similarly, we can never say to God that we have perfectly and completely fulfilled our obligation to love. Specific laws are still needed under this law of love (e.g., "do not murder, do not steal," etc.), but only as a means to an end (cf. John 14:15). Obeying laws just because they are laws and not out of a greater desire to love the Lawgiver is called legalism, which was one of the main problems of the Pharisees, a group of self–righteous Jews so often the target of Jesus's condemnations (see Mt. 23).

As we saw in chapters four and five, in order to safeguard His teachings, Jesus set up the Church (and particularly the papacy) to protect and interpret, under the guidance of the Holy Spirit, His revealed doctrines and moral teachings. The Church doesn't make things up as She goes along, trying to make people's lives miserable. Far from it! The Church is the means by which God Himself wants to lead us to full joy and life with Him by giving us time–tested directions for our lives. Many people today, however, claim that having to obey Church teaching violates their "freedom of conscience." Before we can answer this question, we have to understand just what a "conscience" is.

Conscience is the God–given capacity of a human being to understand the law of God written on the heart of every human being. We have two duties toward our consciences. First, we must *obey* it. You should never disobey your conscience for any reason, since that is a betrayal of your very dignity as a child of God. It is also true, however, that you must properly *inform* it. According to the teaching of the Church, we are to form our consciences in harmony with the Church's Magisterium, the living teaching authority of the Church. As the *Catechism* states:

> In the formation of conscience the Word of God is the light for our path; we must assimilate it in faith and prayer and put it into practice. We must also examine our conscience before the Lord's Cross. We are assisted by the gifts of the Holy Spirit, aided by the witness or advice of others and guided by the authoritative teaching of the Church (*CCC*, #1785).

> As far as possible conscience should take account of the good of all, as expressed in the moral law, natural and revealed, and consequently in the law of the Church and in the authoritative teaching of the Magisterium on moral questions. *Personal conscience and reason should not be set in opposition to the moral law or the Magisterium of the Church* (*CCC*, #2039 – emphasis added).

Thus, consciences are much more than simply our own custom—made moral codes personally tailored to our specifications. Rather, they are to be the reflection of *God's* moral order as we understand it. In order to know right from wrong in specific cases, then, we must turn to those sources God has given us for such knowledge. But what about individual acts? What are considered "sins" and what are not? What are serious sins, according to God and His Church? These are the important questions we will deal with in the next section.

EXERCISE #19: Suppose you are having a discussion with someone who owns slaves. He sincerely believes that black people are not worth as much as whites, and says that his conscience allows him to have slaves. What arguments would you use against him? Discuss this in a small group and write your results in your journal.

The word **"sin"** in Hebrew means "to miss the mark." All sin, essentially, is missing the mark set for us by our loving Father. Our first parents "missed the mark" by committing some sin of prideful disobedience (known as **"original sin"**). **Actual sins** are those actions in which we ourselves freely participate knowing that they are wrong. There are two kinds of actual sin (see 1 John 5:17). **Venial sins** harm, but do not destroy, our relationship with God. These sins, however, are still dangerous since they weaken our defenses against mortal sin and lessen the love of God in our souls and in our world, and thus should be avoided at all costs.

Even more harmful, though, are **mortal ("deadly") sins**. Mortal sins "kill" grace, that share of God's life in your soul, thus separating a person from God. There are three conditions that must be met in order for an action to be considered mortally sinful. First, it must be a serious matter. This is to judged by God and His Church, not by individuals. Even though the law of love is paramount for Christians, there are still lists of specific actions which would keep one out of eternal joy with God (see Mt. 15:19; 1 Cor. 6:9–10; and Eph. 5:5; et. al.). The second criteria for a sin to be considered mortal is sufficient knowledge. In other words, the person committing the sin must know it is seriously wrong. Thirdly, there must be full consent of the will. For example, if you do not freely perform a sinful action (e.g., being forced at gunpoint to rob a convenience store), you are not as responsible for it as if you would have freely done it. Similarly, God only judges us on those things we fully know to be wrong and yet freely do anyway.

It is important to note at this point that human beings do not have the right to judge someone's interior motives or dispositions. While we have a duty to point out conduct that is objectively sinful, we must not, in any way, act as if a particular person is beyond redemption. God alone knows the level of knowledge and consent of the will an individual has, and He alone will be responsible for judging that person.

All sin has far reaching effects. It obscures our vision and can lead to moral blindness, which leads to even more sin. Furthermore, whether we are aware of it or not, punishment for sin is inevitable. God's moral laws, like the laws of nature (gravity, etc.), cannot be broken without a consequence occurring. This is part of God's mercy and justice. Because of His infinite love, He wants to "wake us up" out of our sinfulness so we can change and come back to Him. The temporal effects of our sins must be atoned for either in this life or in the life to come.

To illustrate, let us turn to an example of slander. Suppose your sister is jealous of you for getting a good grade on an exam. She tells her friends that you cheated on it. After awhile, she regrets her action and apologizes. Even after you have forgiven her, there might still be dozens of people who now think less of you because of her false rumor. In order to even begin to truly make up for his sin of slander, she must trace down all those who might have heard it and clear your good name. The same is true of all sin. In order to rebalance the scales of the objective order of creation, justice must be done, and things must be set right. This is the other main reason why some kind of punishment always accompanies sin.

Since the act of sinning tends to breed more sin, certain bad habits can be formed. These bad moral habits are called "vices." Traditionally, there are seven of these known as "capital" sins that have enumerated some of the deadliest personal offenses against God known to man. The capital sin of **pride** is a disordered love of self and an excessive concern for one's own self– esteem or well–being, in which we place ourselves in God's place and forgetting others. Pride is the root of all sin, since whenever we sin we assert that we know better than God. **Lust** is another capital sin, which is defined as a disordered desire for sexual pleasure. **Avarice** is a disordered desire for material possessions, while **envy** represents a disordered desire for the goods of another. The capital sin of **anger** is a disordered desire for revenge, though a Christian can be justifiably angry if it for a just reason (e.g., moral outrage at sin or injustice) and kept under control. **Gluttony** means having a disordered and willful desire for food and/or drink, while **sloth** is a disordered desire for ease, especially in regard to spiritual duties.

Besides committing a sinful act personally, there are also occasions when we might share in the responsibility for the sin of another person by directly or indirectly cooperating with them. For example, it is sinful to order and/or give approval to the sinful action of another. Also, by not revealing or not stopping the sins of another person when we are bound to do so is itself sinful, as is protecting those who do evil.

We must remember that in a sense, we "slap" Christ in the face every time we sin, since we hurt our Creator, Redeemer, and the best Friend we could ever have. As followers of Christ attempting to live out a life of virtue, we must avoid sin not merely because of the punishments that come along as a consequence of the act, but above all because they offend our Lord, who made us out of love and wants us to love Him in return.

EXERCISE #20: Answer the following question and be prepared to discuss it in class: For each of the Seven Capital Sins, come up with an opposite virtue that would satisfactorily reverse the damage of the vice.

In order to help us avoid sin and to live a fully human life, God has given us **grace**, of which we spoke at length in the previous chapter on sacraments. Along with this share of His life in our souls come certain gifts which help us live out this grace. **Virtues** are power from God to accomplish some kind of moral good. At Baptism, the **Three Theological Virtues** are given to us. They are called "theological" because they have God as their source and object.

Faith aims our intellects at God and His truth, and helps us to believe in what He has revealed to us through Christ and His Church.

Since "faith without works is dead" (see James 2:26), believers must always be witnessing for ways to live out their faith as well as spread it. The virtue of supernatural faith is a free gift to all those who seek it, the means by which we begin to live with God (see John 17:3), and the manner in which God gives a right direction to our present life.

The Old Testament holds up the example of faith given by Abraham, whom the Catholic Church acknowledges as "our father in faith." God revealed Himself to Abraham, who unhesitatingly obeyed, even when severely tested. The New Testament offers the faithful witness of the Blessed Virgin Mary. Her response to the Archangel Gabriel at the Annunciation, which made possible the redemption of mankind, has served as the perfect model of a humble and obedient faith for Christians throughout the history of the Church.

Growth in the virtue of faith can happen in many different ways. We must first of all pray to God for a more mature faith, confident that He will hear us. We may also more carefully attend to the Word of God as it is offered to us through the Sacred Scriptures and through the teaching authority of the Catholic Church. Since our faith has an intellectual dimension to it, we must always study our faith to get an ever deeper appreciation for its beauty and richness. Growth in this virtue is also accomplished by cultivating relationships with people of faith. This can be done not only by reading and praying over the lives of the saints, but also by forging friendships with people striving to be holy in today's world.

The theological virtue of **hope** opens the will to God, and helps us desire and confidently strive for eternal life. This virtue helps guide us to our true home, where we will be perfectly happy. Thus, hope helps to prevent us from two extremes. On the one hand, hope helps us not give in to despair, when a person no longer trusts that God will save him or her or will fulfill His promises. Authentic Christian hope prevents us from becoming discouraged or from abandoning the firm trust we have in Christ. On the other hand, living the virtue of hope keeps us from the other extreme of presumption, which effectively denies hope by placing too much reliance on a person's individual powers (e.g., expecting to save oneself by one's own merits, absolutely demanding God answer a prayer request in a particular way, etc.). The virtue of hope affects our lives on a deeper level than that of simply emotion. In other words, Christians full of hope do not always walk around with painted smiles on their faces. Rather, they live with the firm conviction of mind and heart that Jesus is Lord, and nothing ultimately falls outside the plan of God.

The highest theological virtue, though, is **love** (see 1 Cor. 13:1–13). The word "love" is often used in today's society, but not always in the sense in which it is used here. The ancient Greeks spoke of four types of love: storge (natural affection or liking), eros (sexual desire), philia (friendship), and agape (selfless love). Agape is the type of love meant by this third Theological virtue, and is sometimes translated as "charity." Regardless of the name by which we refer to it, the virtue of love is the essence of the Christian life.

The selfless love of Christ on the cross is the model for all Christian love, and is the driving force and inspiration behind all of the other virtues. If our relationship with Christ is only on the level of avoiding punishment or seeking rewards, we are missing one of the most important opportunities of our lives—to live as children of God Himself. Our main concern in the moral life should be to best respond in love to the One who has first loved us (see 1 John 4:19).

The moral life also hinges on what the *Catechism* refers to as "human virtues." Chief among all the human virtues that help human beings lead happy, well-balanced lives, four have traditionally held to be the ones on which a good moral life "hinges", and are thus called the **Cardinal Virtues** ("cardo" means "hinge" in Latin).

The first of these four virtues is called **prudence**. This virtue helps us to know and choose God's will, and enables us to make good, prayerful decisions. The prudent person avoids rushing into situations or making quick judgments without thinking clearly. The prudent person also avoids agonizing unnecessarily over choices, and is not paralyzed when making a decision. This virtue will not only help you make major life choices (e.g., vocation, career, etc.), but also is an indispensable aid when deciding everyday things: Should I go out with this person? Should I go to this party or avoid it? How should I talk to my friend about her family problems?

Justice is the virtue that helps us respect the rights of God and other human beings by giving them what is their due. Living justly means we treat other people with the dignity they deserve as children of God. It also means fulfilling our duties we have been given as members of the Church, the family of God. The virtue of **fortitude** helps to courageously pursue the will of God and to steadfastly endure whatever trials come our way in our pursuit of what is good. Fortitude acts as a balance between the two extremes of foolhardiness and fear. Many of the martyrs of the Church provide us with excellent examples of fortitude in action. While not relishing the thought of a painful death, they did not let fear paralyze them when it came time for them to offer their witness to

Christ and His Church. Jesus Himself offers us the perfect witness of fortitude in the Garden of Gethsemane. While not directly provoking His enemies into killing Him, Our Lord did not shrink from fulfilling His mission, even when faced with fierce hatred.

The fourth cardinal virtue, **temperance**, helps us to moderate our wants and control our instincts. Persons who are temperate are able to enjoy the good and beautiful things that God has created, avoiding the misuse and abuse of His gifts. Temperate people are able to enjoy food, drink, periods of rest, and other benefits this life has to offer us without becoming gluttonous, drunk, or lazy. Growth in all four of these cardinal virtues is accomplished with learning more about them, observing the witness of people who exemplify them, the process of trying to live them out, and, above all else, divine grace.

The **Seven Gifts of the Holy Spirit**, also given at Baptism, are drawn out in a special way at Confirmation (see Isaiah 11:2–3). These gifts, spoken of at greater length in chapter 12, help us to live the life of a true Christian in today's world, which can be a great challenge.

Thus, even though our human nature is tainted by the effects of original sin and tends toward sinful acts, God has been very generous in helping us live lives that will be truly happy, healthy, and holy. In the next few chapters, we will examine many different issues and see how they relate to your efforts at living a Christian life.

EXERCISE #21: In your journals, answer the following questions: Which one of the Three Theological Virtues do you need most right now in your life and why? Which one of the Four Cardinal Virtues do you need most in your life right now and why? Which one of the Gifts of the Holy Spirit do you need most in your life right now and why?

CHAPTER SEVENTEEN

LOVE OF GOD

Jesus said, "If you love me, keep my commandments" (John 14:15). In saying this, Our Lord is not ordering us to have "warm fuzzy feelings" about Almighty God. Rather, we are called to "love" God by perfectly and humbly obeying what He has invited us to do—serve Him and those around us. That is the essence of a true love for God, and on that basis we will be judged (see Mt. 25:31–46).

The first three commandments have to do with our relationship with God Himself. The first commandment says that "I am the Lord your God. You shall not have other gods besides Me" (Ex. 20:2–6, Dt. 5:1–10). The second commandment, which flows from the first, says "You shall not take the name of the Lord, your God, in vain" (Ex. 20:7, Dt. 5:11). The third commands that everyone must "keep holy the Lord's Day" (Ex 20:8–11, Dt. 5:15).

These commandments help people to focus only on God in their lives and to give Him what is His due as Creator of the Universe. Thus, we are urged to have no other gods besides Him. Having false gods is not as uncommon as it might sound. Anytime we put someone (rock stars, movie stars, sports stars, etc.) or something (money, power, sex, pleasure, science, etc.) in God's place, we commit idolatry, a serious sin against this commandment. Likewise, any time we seriously consult astrologers (via horoscopes), spirits of the dead (via ouija boards), or show disrespect to God or something holy (called "sacrilege") in some way, we are violating one of the minimum standards required for a good relationship with the Lord.

One of the best ways to honor this commandment is to pray often and well. Communication between human beings and God can take many forms. Worshipping God as Creator and Redeemer of all, thanking

Him for all His gifts, and voluntarily sacrificing certain goods for the love of Him are very good examples of ways to keep the first of these three commandments.

The second commandment urges us to use God's gift of speech correctly, and to never use the power of words wrongly. Blasphemy can be defined as any speech or thought which shows contempt for God or His Church. Cursing is calling down evil on someone or something in God's Name. We must also remember to not use God's name in vain or irreverently; that is, without good reason or proper respect. Even if we have developed a bad habit of doing this, we must work every day to break the habit, always relying on the grace of God for help. Just as we pay attention to someone who is speaking to us in conversation (especially someone "important!"), so should we make sure we are paying attention to God when we pray. The essence of the second commandment is to use the gift of speech God gave us to serve Him faithfully.

In the third commandment, God has made it quite clear that He wants us to remember Him and be with Him in a special way at least once a week. We accomplish this by reverently assisting at Mass on Sundays and Holy Days. Skipping Mass for no good reason knowingly and willfully, or just "showing up" in body and not in spirit does not fulfill our obligation in terms of this commandment. Imagine going out to supper with someone who stares off into space instead of looking at you, doesn't listen to you or take part in the conversation, and is constantly and impatiently looking at his watch. If acting like that at a dinner is inappropriate, how much more so at Mass.

The invitation to worship God one day a week is not all that difficult to accept. After all, everyone is aware of how much we need "breaks" in our lives. In order not to become too busy for God, He has decreed that we set aside one day a week for rest, recreation with family and friends, and for renewal of body and soul. Without this time, we become less and less human and more and more like robots.

We can easily see, then, the wonderful wisdom behind each of these commandments so far. God is commanding us to do things that are really for our own benefit in the long run. By keeping these first three commandments, we are giving clear testimony to our love for God.

EXERCISE #22: In your journals, answer the following questions: Do you have any idols, things which rival or even surpass God in terms of your time, resources, and interest? Is Sunday any different (in terms of your relationship with God) than any other day of the week?

CHAPTER EIGHTEEN

THE DOMESTIC CHURCH

As we have seen, the first three commandments deal with our relationship with God. The last seven commandments have to do with our relationships with other human beings. The link between the first three and the rest of these divine commands is the fourth commandment: "Honor your father and your mother" (Ex. 20:12; Dt. 5:16).

God was certainly not obligated to create families. He could have continued the human race in any way He wished. It is important to reflect on, then, why He has ordered that a man and woman come together for life to help create and nurture new life. One of the main principles of this commandment is that God is the source for all true authority, including parental authority. In obeying and honoring your parents, you show your respect for the order of creation God has established. To show the dignity of the family, the Church has repeatedly called the family "the domestic Church," for it is within this most basic human community that we first learn about the love of God and life within His family.

In order to keep this commandment, children must obey, respect, and take care of their parents when they are old. Most of all, children should pray for their parents (see Pr. 30:17; Sir. 3:1–16; 1 Tim. 5:4). Parents, too, have obligations with regard to this commandment. They are bound to provide for their children's bodily and spiritual needs, to respect God's authority by not obstructing the will of God in the lives of their children, and to teach their children well in word and deed and, when necessary, imposing reasonable correction and punishment.

Children are often highly critical of parents. The reverse is also true at times. It is crucial to keep in mind, though, that parenting is an extremely difficult and awesome task, one for which "how–to" manuals are rarely provided. Sometimes your parents might make mistakes in the process of raising you, just as you might make some mistakes in the process of growing up. Even though it is almost inevitable that during your adolescence conflicts will arise between you and your parents, it is not inevitable that these conflicts have to end in bitterness and anger. If both children and parents are serious about keeping this commandment, family life is much more healthy and pleasant.

For example, suppose you and your mother and father have a disagreement about your plans for the weekend. You and your parents almost certainly share a desire to have you enjoy time with your friends as well as a desire to make sure that you are safe. Thus, you really do start off the discussion on common ground, and the real subject of the discussion ought to be how to balance these goals. You both probably want to avoid two extremes. One extreme position is that your parents would have no expectations of you whatsoever; you could date a neo–Nazi, rob banks, and smoke marijuana in church buildings and they wouldn't mind a bit. The other extreme would be a jail–type atmosphere where you would have no freedom or responsibility for your own actions. The tricky part comes in trying to decide on a balance.

You, as the son or daughter, ought to operate with the love asked of you by Our Lord in the fourth commandment by respectfully discussing this with your parents, conducting yourself in a mature manner. Your parents, for their part, ought to be reasonable and loving. Whatever their decision, you should respectfully obey it, knowing that you will be held accountable for the way which you treated the parents God gave you. If you truly believe your parents to be wrong, you have two options. One is to disobey them, thereby risking punishment, a further decline in your relationship, and offending God. The other is to make clear that you disagree with them, but that you will submit to their decision anyway out of respect for them.

It is fairly obvious that family life has taken a severe beating in this latter part of the 20th century. The lives of many families have been broken by divorce, alcoholism, abuse, or by a deadly lack of honest and open communication. Many young people become painfully aware at very young ages of the faults of their parents, and suffer greatly because of it. But just because your parents do not or cannot keep up their end of this commandment does not mean you would be better off by not keeping your end.

There is no doubt that Our Loving Lord stands by those in such difficult circumstances. We can always turn to Him for help, and He is ever there, placing trusted friends, teachers, relatives, clergy, coaches, counse-

Our Lady of Perpetual Help,
pray for us

lors, etc. in our path to help us in those situations. No teenager should ever think that they are responsible for their parents' problems or that they have to solve them by themselves. Young adults have enough on their minds with school and relationships, let alone trying to keep their parents' marriage together or helping them stay sober. Thus, parents must never invoke the fourth commandment as a means of forcing a child to "cover up" sinful situations.

Whether your family is beset with large or small problems, you can do your part by honoring your mother and father in the best way possible, and by praying for them every day. The Church has always held up the witness of the members of the Holy Family, and we may pray to Jesus, Mary, and Joseph to help our families and for assistance in keeping this important commandment.

EXERCISE #23: Think of two faults you believe your parents suffer from. Now think of two of your own faults. How are they the same? How are they different? How many times have you apologized to your parents in the last week for one of your faults?

CHAPTER NINETEEN

RESPECT FOR LIFE

One of God's greatest gifts to mankind is life itself. Burning with an eternal desire to give of Himself, God "breathed" life into the first man (see Gen. 2:7) and ever since has provided for the growth and increase of the human family. The Church teaches that God has a plan for each and every human being, and passionately desires that we share eternal life and joy with Him in heaven.

In order that earthly societies might reflect the beauty of this gift of life, God made known to man one of the most basic human laws of any society. This law has been preserved in the fifth commandment: "You shall not kill" (Ex. 20:13; Dt. 5:17). This commandment prohibits the killing of innocent human life, but Jesus extends it and prohibits that which leads to murder—uncontrolled or unjustifiable anger (see Mt. 5:21–22).

There are many ways our society shows a fundamental disregard for the living, and in order to truly guard against the taking of innocent human life, all Catholics must be made aware of a number of life issues.

One of the foremost human rights issues of our time is undoubtedly that of **abortion**. The Catholic Church has taught authoritatively that direct abortion is the deliberate murder of an innocent human being and is totally immoral, no matter what the circumstances. Many people in our society strongly disagree, and the current law of the land in the U.S. allows for this slaughter to continue, with approximately 4,000 abortions being performed *every day*. Yet Catholics must resist this holocaust, since the murder of a child by his or her own mother destroys not only the life of both the mother and child, but the society as well which allows this to happen. It is vitally important that all Catholics do something to stop abortion, though individual circumstances will dictate just what particular course to take (e.g., prayer, letter writing, political work, etc.). Young adults can and should offer the Church the awesome gift of their energy, hope, and enthusiasm in the struggle to protect the unborn. Christ promised to ask us how we treated Him when He was most vulnerable, and there is no one else in the world more vulnerable today than a child in his or her mother's womb.

Another common social issue that relates to the fifth commandment as well as to the life of young adults is that of **suicide**. The act of suicide is obviously gravely sinful, since it destroys the gift of life God has given a person. Only God can tell whether or not an individual would go to hell for committing suicide, though, since only God can judge whether the person knew it was seriously wrong and how freely they committed the act. Most psychologists say that people who attempt suicide are emotionally distraught individuals who are really looking for a way out of what appears to them to be an impossible situation. Thus, one must be very cautious when dealing with people who are threatening or seriously contemplating suicide. One should immediately obtain some kind of help from individuals familiar with counseling suicidal people (e.g., counselors, teachers, clergy, etc.), since they have or can obtain the expertise necessary for such a serious job.

If a friend ever tells you he or she is thinking seriously about suicide, one of the most important things you can do is listen. Comforting those in need is a great act of love, and letting the person know there is help can be a tremendous service to them. Even if they tell you to tell no one else, the very fact they are speaking with you is a veiled cry for help, and you should not feel guilty for getting some outside assistance.

Closely related to the tragedy of suicide is the sin of **euthanasia**, also known as "mercy killing." Since God alone is the author of life, it is gravely immoral to directly and willfully take it from handicapped, sick, or dying persons (cf. *CCC*, #2276–2279).

The **illegal or excessive use of drugs and alcohol** is also a serious sin against this commandment, since by either intentionally damaging one's body or impairing the operation of one's mind and will, a person mistreats God's sacred gift of life. The same is true of intentionally **risking one's life** or the lives of others unnecessarily (e.g., reckless driving, etc.). Also falling under this category of serious sins against life is the sin of **neglect**, both of oneself and of others entrusted to your care. An eating disorder such as anorexia nervosa or bulimia is an example of conduct that is objectively seriously sinful. Though it is unclear just how responsible some of these people are for their actions, it is an insult to God to voluntarily starve oneself to the point of serious sickness or even death in order to "improve" one's physical appearance.

Similarly, if we neglect those who suffer as a result of poverty and natural disasters, the Church teaches us that we are, in a real way, responsible for their deaths. Never to be mindful of and never to help the poor in a material way would be a serious violation of Jesus' law of love (see Luke 16:19–31). Members of the Catholic Church must always be vigilant in helping to respect the life of God in their brothers and sisters, in order to show the world the awesome love of God.

EXERCISE #24: Working in small groups, write in your notebooks your answers to the following cases:

A. Mark, a fairly good friend of yours, has recently been cut from the basketball team, dumped by his girlfriend, and has just failed an important Geometry exam. His life seems to be unravelling, and he confesses to you that he wishes he could just end it all. List five concrete things you could do for him that would help him not take his life.

B. You notice Sue, a close friend, has lost over 20 pounds in the last month. Although some of your friends are telling her she looks nice, you note she is much paler than usual and noticeably weaker. You then see her making herself vomit in the bathroom. List five concrete things you could do for Sue that show your concern for her life and health.

C. Your cousin Jean gets drunk every time you out to parties and is otherwise constantly sneaking drinks in and out of school. Her drinking has affected her school work and her whole personality. You know she drives home from school drunk every afternoon and you are afraid for her and for anyone she might hurt. List five concrete things you could do on Jean's behalf.

CHAPTER TWENTY

CHASTITY

Closely related to God's command for us to respect the gift of life is His command to respect His gift of sexuality and the power to create new life. Once again, God shows us the absolutely mind–boggling amount of respect He has for human beings by actually asking us to help Him create other human beings through the proper exercise of sexual love. The sixth ("You shall not commit adultery") and ninth ("You shall not covet your neighbor's wife") commandments (see Ex. 20:14,17; Dt. 5:18,21) help us understand what exactly God expects of us in regard to sexual morality.

Our Lord expects all of His followers to live the virtue of **chastity**; that is, to offer to God the gift of our sexuality (see Mt. 19:1–12). This only makes sense, since it means "following the directions" that God the Creator, the "Inventor" of sexuality, has sent along with this wonderful gift.

Chastity is lived in a number of ways by different people. Married people live the virtue of chastity by pledging to share sexual love exclusively with each other for the rest of their lives. Single people are called to live chastely by saving for marriage the awesome power at their disposal. Priests and religious take a vow of chastity, which means they set aside their right to marry and have children for the greater good of the Church and out of love for Christ.

Contrary to much of what our society believes, it is a simple fact that our body is not exclusively ours. We did not make our own bodies, nor, as St. Paul taught, must we think we can live only for ourselves (see 1 Corinthians. 6:18–20). Because of this, the Church teaches that sex is a beautiful gift from God (see Gen. 1:27–28), and is not bad unless we misuse it in some way.

It is clear that much of our society advocates the absolute "free" practice of sex, and views the teaching on sexuality outlined in this chapter as ridiculous or unrealistic. What is truly "unrealistic," however, is thinking that by arrogantly dismissing the dictates of the Author of sexuality, we may make sex "better." One of the saddest sights in modern times is the large number of people absolutely enslaved to their sexual passions. Far from being "free," they reel from one sexual experience to another, barely living above the level of animals. Human beings neither invented sex nor give meaning to the act. Suppose you go to a restaurant and instead of offering the clerk money for your purchase of pizza, you give her six sheets of toilet paper. She would obviously reject your offer, because you do not have the authority to give toilet paper any value as money. Only the government can make and issue money, for many good reasons. In the same way, human beings have no authority to give a different meaning to the gift of sexuality than its Creator did.

God not only has given meaning to sex, but has decreed through the teaching authority of His Church that the two main purposes of sex are **procreation** and **unity**. Procreation means being open to children, and unity means giving oneself to another in love. Both purposes are essentially unselfish, since they are directed at others, and can only be fulfilled in marriage.

Any misuse of the sexual act boils down to a selfish use of sex and of other people. Thus, a true understanding of authentic sexual love means that we not misuse it in any number of ways. In general, having sex with someone who is not your spouse, known as **fornication**, is objectively a serious moral wrong and is specifically noted as one of the sins that can exclude one from heaven (see 1 Corinthians. 6:9–10). This includes not only **adultery** (when a person has sex with someone else's spouse), but **premarital sex** as well.

Further, since **homosexual acts** are by definition incapable of both procreation and a true exchange between persons, they are grossly immoral. This does not necessarily mean, however, that people with a homosexual orientation are all going to hell or deserve to be ridiculed. The reason why certain people are physically attracted to members of their own sex is not fully understood. Nevertheless, the Church teaches that a homosexual orientation is "disordered," and that homosexual acts cannot be assumed as a "right" in which people may indulge. People with a homosexual orientation must be treated with the respect that all human beings deserve, and should be counseled and supported as they strive to live chaste lives.

EXERCISE #25: Working in small groups, write in your notebooks a list of all the possible effects ("negative" as well as "positive") of a sexually promiscuous life during high school.

This section of this chapter on living the virtue of chastity deals with the crucial issue of **dating**. Having sound relationships with people of the opposite sex is a critically important part of your process of growing into adulthood. For some people, dating comes naturally, early, and often. For others, dating comes later or infrequently. While many people think that the first option is better, it is not necessarily so. For many reasons it is often particularly unwise to get into a serious dating relationship at a young age. Many healthy people never date at all in high school, or go out in groups of friends of both sexes. It is often best to follow the advice and direction of noted experts in this area, people who know you, love you and who are totally dedicated to your welfare—say, for example, your parents.

Young people who are strong and courageous enough to be faithful followers of Christ should follow certain basic principles when dating seriously. First, you should keep in mind that actions that bring about sexual stimulation through physical touch are reserved for marriage. Obviously, there is nothing wrong with holding hands or certain other types of exchanges of affection. A general rule of thumb to remember is this: Before you engage in some kind of activity, imagine that Christ, the Blessed Mother, and your parents are watching you. This should not frighten you into frigidity, but encourage you to be the best person you can be at all times as well as prevent you from getting hurt. While it is unlikely your parents will be watching you on dates, it is certain that God will be.

Our Lord was quite clear about our duty to reject even lustful thoughts and desires (see Mt. 5:27–30). Thus, any type of **pornography** is certainly out of place for one who proclaims to follow the Lord of life. Whether in magazine or movie form, pornography degrades both the user the one used. Men and women who use porn to deliberately indulge in lustful fantasies insult the One who designed and fashioned the beautiful human body. The men and women who sell their bodies for use by others are the other victims of porn, in that they allow themselves to be exploited and treated as something less than the truly beautiful human being God intends them to be.

It is difficult to even live in our society today without facing many sexual temptations. Television shows, advertisements, and fashions of dress can all be the occasions for a sexual thought to come to one's mind. Here we must make the careful distinction between a having a temptation and giving into temptation. Everyone, including Christ Himself, is tempted to sin (see Mt. 4:1–11). Yet no one, relying on the grace of God, has to give in to temptation. When sinful thoughts come to mind, we can either dismiss them and thereby refuse sin, or deliberately take pleasure in them, which then involves us in sin. God gives us a choice, and it is up to us to respond faithfully or not.

The last major issue which we will deal with in this chapter on chastity is that of **contraception**. There are many forms of artificial contraception available these days, all of which in some way change the nature of the sex act and by definition deny the possibility of a new life from forming.

The rationale behind the Church's teaching that the use of artificial contraception is morally wrong is twofold. Basically, contraception denies both of the purposes of sexual love. While the procreative purpose of sexual love is obviously denied, so too is the unitive purpose of marital love. Sexual intercourse between a husband and a wife represents a total and true self– giving, and one that is denied by the presence of foreign objects or chemicals that change the very nature of the act.

The procreative and unitive aspects of married love simply cannot be separated. Separating the pleasure that is associated with the sexual act from its other purposes is like an eating disorder, in which a person separates the pleasure of eating from its other purposes like nutrition, socialization, etc. The Church teaches that even married couples who practice contraception commit a great moral evil, and contribute in a very real way to the destruction of a true, loving relationship.

The Church does not teach, however, that couples must throw themselves on nature and have as many children as is humanly possible during the years in which they are able to have children. The *Catechism* allows that "for just reasons, spouses may wish to space the births of their children" (CCC, #2368), provided that they are not motivated by selfishness and that they make use only of moral methods of birth regulation such as "natural family planning," in which the couple abstains from sexual intercourse during those days of the woman's cycle in which she is fertile.

EXERCISE #26: Working in small groups, go back to the place in your notebooks where you completed exercise #25, in which you noted the "positive" and "negative" effects of a sexually promiscuous life. Cross out any of the items on your list which can be *definitely* ruled out as a result of the use of contraceptives.

CHAPTER TWENTY-ONE

STEWARDS OF HIS GIFTS

This chapter will cover those commandments that deal with acting as proper stewards or caretakers of the many gifts God has given us. The seventh commandment, "You shall not steal" (Ex. 20:15; Dt. 5:19), and the tenth commandment, "You shall not covet your neighbor's goods" (Ex. 20:17; Dt. 5:21), are linked in that they call us to use material possessions as God intends and not fall into the trap of making them the most important things in our lives.

The sin of **stealing** involves taking something that does not belong to you without permission. Besides the obvious cases of late night burgling or **shoplifting**, theft is also involved in the case of someone who "finds" something but makes no effort at finding out who the real owner is. **Vandalism** is also a sin against this commandment, since in destroying the property of another you in effect take it away from him or her. **Cheating**, a constant temptation for those in school, is also a form of theft and is always morally wrong. The act is still wrong even if the one who is cheating obtains the person's "permission" before copying the answers to a test or assignment, because then it is a lie, since you are stating or implying that the work is your own when in fact it is not.

Another gift that God gave us which He expects us to put into His service is that of human speech. The eighth commandment, "You shall not bear false witness" (Ex. 20:16; Dt. 5:20), is designed to remind us of this obligation. The disciples of Jesus are to imitate He who is Truth incarnate in being truthful in all that they do, including but not limited only to matters of speech (see James 3:1–12).

The Church teaches that **lies** are evil because they represent a betrayal of the power of the spoken word God, in His wisdom and love, shared with mankind. He certainly did not have to give us the gift of speech, but since He did, we should carefully use this tremendous power for His purposes. We are not required, however, to always divulge everything we know. It is not sinful to withhold information from those who have no right to know (e.g., gang members in search of someone in hiding). It is sinful, however, to withhold information or deliberately mislead people who do have a right to know (e.g., parents asking their children about their whereabouts).

One of the more common abuses of the spoken word in high school is the **gossip** or idle talk about others. While some kinds of gossip are relatively harmless, others can be extremely destructive. A good criterion for judging whether or not something is gossip is asking if the hearer has a *need to know*. If the person(s) involved have no need to know, particularly in regard to sensitive information, then it usually can be judged to be gossip and should be avoided.

Slander is a sin we commit when we speak of the faults of others with the intent to harm their reputation or character. One kind of slander is called **detraction**, where we inappropriately or uncharitably spread things other people have really done. What we say is true, but it is still unnecessarily harmful to another's reputation. For example, suppose a friend confides in you that she had to go through chemical dependency treatment over the summer and is now fully recovered. In order to get back at her for something, you tell a group of friends without asking her for her consent first. **Calumny** is another type of slander that represents an even greater sin, since in this case what is said about another person is actually untrue. As an example, we can turn to the case of a guy in a boy's locker room after baseball practice. When asked how his date was last night, he proceeds to tell a string of lies in order to get the other guys to think he is cool. In so doing, he has damaged the reputation of the girl, and is guilty of a serious offense against God.

In sum, we can see how much God loves each and every human being. In order to help us be truly happy forever, He has given us light posts to light our way on the journey through life back to Him. Just as the Creed helps us understand Who it is we follow, and just as the sacraments give us the grace to bring us closer to Him, so the commandments are His instructions on how best to live this life He has given us.

EXERCISE #27: In your journal, answer the following questions: Have you ever had people talk about you behind your back? How did it feel? Were you able to forgive them?

CHAPTER TWENTY-TWO

CONVERSING WITH CHRIST

In this final chapter, we will turn our attention to the fourth and final section of the *Catechism of the Catholic Church*, which deals with the subject of prayer. The *Catechism* quotes the great Church Father St. John Damascene as it defines prayer: "Prayer is the raising of one's mind and heart to God or the requesting of good things from God" (*CCC*, #2559).

Prayer is a gift from God, who, because of His great love, is constantly calling and inviting each one of us to this mysterious encounter with Himself. Our teacher in prayer is Jesus Christ, who modeled perfect adherence to the will of the Father and showed complete confidence in being heard. The Holy Spirit, teacher and protector of the Church of God, also teaches the followers of Jesus how to pray. And Mary, because of her unique cooperation with the working of the Holy Spirit in the redemption of mankind, is offered to us by God both as a vivid example of a life lived in deep prayer as well as our mother in the order of grace. Thus, "we can pray with her and to her" (*CCC*, #2679).

Our education in prayer is to begin with our families, those "domestic churches" that make up the larger family of God on earth and in heaven, the Church. As we grow older, we are given more guides as well as more opportunities for growing in prayer: teachers help us pray in school, friends and relatives pray with us in a variety of settings, and priests lead us in prayer during liturgical celebrations.

There are three major ways Christians have expressed the life of prayer: **vocal prayer**, **meditation**, and **contemplative prayer**. Since we have both bodies and souls, external prayer that expresses in physical speech the internal prayers of our heart, is a very important part of the Christian life. Furthermore, vocal prayer also makes it easier for us to join our brothers and sisters in common adoration, petition, thanksgiving, and praise of God. Meditation is a quest of the mind and heart to understand and apply in one's own life the infinite richness of the Gospel message. Certain types of music, art, books, or prayers (e.g., the rosary) can all help us in sound meditation that aims at turning our hearts more and more to God.

Contemplative prayer, however, is aimed at nothing less than *union with God*. It is, in the words of St. Teresa of Avila, "a close sharing between friends; it means taking time frequently to be alone with him who we know loves us" (CCC, #2709). Christians seeking to grow in contemplative prayer will *make* time for the Lord, setting aside regular time for conversation with our loving Father in heaven who loves us beyond all telling and who has forgiven us beyond our wildest hopes. Contemplative prayer also means being attentive to the Word of God as it comes to us in our daily lives; it is a gift from God that furthers a most intense kind of covenant relationship and communion with Him. The more we pray contemplatively, the more we become like God, and the more we become ready to live with Him and all the saints forever in heaven.

EXERCISE #28: In your journal, answer the following questions: Which of the three expressions of prayer do you practice most – vocal prayer, meditation, or contemplative prayer? Where? Why? How could you increase the time spent in the other forms of prayer?

APOSTLES' CREED (CREDO): I believe in God, the Father almighty, creator of heaven and earth; and in Jesus Christ, his only Son, our Lord. He was conceived by power of the Holy Spirit, and was born of the Virgin Mary. He suffered under Pontius Pilate, was crucified, died, and was buried. He descended into hell. On the third day He rose again. He ascended into heaven and is seated at the right hand of the Father. He will come again to judge the living and the dead. I believe in the Holy Spirit, the holy catholic Church, the communion of saints, the forgiveness of sins, the resurrection of the body, and life everlasting. Amen.

OUR FATHER (PATER NOSTER): Our Father, who art in heaven, hallowed be Thy name; Thy Kingdom come, Thy will be done on earth as it is in heaven. Give us this day our daily bread; and forgive us our trespasses as we forgive those who trespass against us; and lead us not into temptation but deliver us from evil. Amen.

HAIL MARY (AVE MARIA): Hail Mary, full of grace; the Lord is with thee; blessed art thou among women, and blessed is the fruit of thy womb, Jesus. Holy Mary, Mother of God, pray for us sinners, now and at the hour of our death. Amen.

GLORY BE (GLORIA): Glory be to the Father, and to the Son, and to the Holy Spirit; as it was in the beginning, is now, and ever shall be, world without end. Amen.

HAIL, HOLY QUEEN (SALVE REGINA): Hail, Holy Queen, Mother of Mercy. Hail our life, our sweetness and our hope. To thee do we cry, poor banished children of Eve. To thee do we send up our sighs; mourning and weeping in this vale of tears. Turn then, most gracious advocate, thine eyes of mercy toward us; and after this our exile, show unto us the blessed fruit of thy womb, Jesus. O clement, O loving, O sweet Virgin Mary.

ACT OF FAITH: O my God, I firmly believe that Thou art one God in three divine Persons, Father, Son, and Holy Spirit. I believe that Thy divine Son became man, died for our sins, and that He will come to judge the living and the dead. I believe these and all the truths which the Holy Catholic Church teaches, because Thou hast revealed them, who can neither deceive nor be deceived. Amen.

ACT OF HOPE: O my God, relying on Thy almighty power and infinite mercy and promises, I hope to obtain pardon of my sins, the help of Thy grace, and life everlasting through the merits of Jesus Christ, my Lord and Redeemer. Amen.

ACT OF LOVE: O my God, I love Thee above all things, with my whole heart and soul, because Thou art all–good and worthy of all love. I love my neighbor as myself for the love of Thee. I forgive all who have injured me, and ask pardon of all whom I have injured. Amen.

AN ACT OF CONTRITION: O my God, I am heartily sorry for having offended Thee. I detest all my sins because I dread the loss of heaven and the pains of hell, but most of all because they offend Thee, my God, Who art all good and deserving of all my love. I firmly resolve, with the help of Thy grace, to sin no more and to avoid the near occasions of sin. Amen.

MEMORARE: Remember, O most gracious Virgin Mary that never was it known that anyone who fled to thy protection, implored thy help, or sought thy intercession was left unaided. Inspired by this confidence, I fly to thee O Virgin of virgins, my mother. To thee I come; before thee I stand, sinful and sorrowful. O Mother of the Word Incarnate, despise not my petitions, but in thy mercy, hear and answer me. Amen.

ANGEL OF GOD: Angel of God, My Guardian Dear, to whom His love commits me here, ever this day be at my side, to light and guard, to rule and guide. Amen.

COME, HOLY SPIRIT: Come, Holy Spirit, fill the hearts of Thy faithful and enkindle in them the fire of Thy love.

– Send forth Thy Spirit, O Lord, and they shall be created,

Response: and Thou shalt renew the face of the earth. Amen.

FATIMA PRAYER: O my Jesus, forgive us our sins. Save us from the fires of Hell. Lead all souls to heaven, especially those in most need of Thy mercy. (to be said at the end of each decade of the rosary)

*"And behold, I am with you always, yes,
even until the end of time" (see Matthew 28:20).*

ST. MICHAEL THE ARCHANGEL: St. Michael the Archangel, defend us in the day of battle. Be our safeguard against the wickedness and snares of the devil. Rebuke him, we humbly pray, and do thou, O prince of the heavenly host, by the power of God, cast into Hell Satan and all the other evil spirits who prowl through the world, seeking the ruin of souls. Amen. (Pope Leo XIII)

MORNING OFFERING: O Jesus, through the Immaculate Heart of Mary, I offer Thee all my prayers, works, joys, and sufferings of this day in union with the Holy Sacrifice of the Mass throughout the world. I offer them for all the intentions of Thy Sacred Heart; the salvation of souls, reparation for sin, the reunion of all Christians. I offer them for the intentions of our bishops and of all apostles of prayer, and in particular for those recommended by our Holy Father this month. Amen.

ANIMA CHRISTI: Soul of Christ, be my sanctification. Body of Christ, be my salvation. Blood of Christ, fill all my veins. Water of Christ's side, wash out all my stains. Passion of Christ, my comfort be. O good Jesus, listen to me. In Thy wounds I fain would hide, never to be parted from Thy side. Guard me should the foe assail me, call me when my life shall fail me. Bid me come to Thee above, with Thy saints to sing Thy love, world without end. Amen. (trans. by J.H. Cardinal Newman)

BEFORE MEAL PRAYER: Bless us, O Lord, and these, Thy gifts, which we are about to receive from Thy bounty, through Christ, our Lord. Amen.

AFTER MEAL PRAYER: We give Thee thanks, Almighty God, for these and all Thy blessings, which we have received from Thy bounty, through Christ, our Lord. Amen. May the souls of the faithful departed, through the mercy of God, rest in peace. Amen.

ANGELUS:

– The angel of the Lord declared unto Mary...

Response: ... and she conceived by the Holy Spirit. (Hail Mary)

– Behold the handmaid of the Lord...

R: ... be it done unto me according to your word. (Hail Mary)

– And the word was made flesh...

R: ... and dwelt among us. (Hail Mary)

– Pray for us, O Holy Mother of God...

R: ... that we may be made worthy of the promises of Christ.

– Let us pray. Pour forth thy grace into our hearts, O Lord. By the message of the angel we have learned of the incarnation of Christ, Thy Son. Lead us, by His Passion and Cross, to the glory of the Resurrection, through the same Christ, Our Lord.

R: Amen.

QUEEN OF HEAVEN: (Angelus during Eastertide)

– Queen of heaven, rejoice, Alleluia.

Response: The Son whom thou were privileged to bear, Alleluia,

– has risen as He said, Alleluia.

R: Pray to God for us, Alleluia.

– Rejoice and be glad, Virgin Mary, Alleluia.

R: For the Lord has truly risen, Alleluia.

– Let us pray. O God, it was by the Resurrection of Thy Son, our Lord Jesus Christ, that Thou brought joy to the world. Grant that through the intercession of the Virgin Mary, His Mother, we may attain the joy of eternal life, through Christ, Our Lord. Amen.

PRAYER FOR THE FAITHFUL DEPARTED:

– Eternal rest grant unto them, O Lord.

Response: And let the perpetual light shine upon them.

– May their souls and the souls of all the faithful departed, through the mercy of God, rest in peace.

R: Amen.

PRAYER FOR SCHOLARS (BY ST. THOMAS AQUINAS)

Grant me, most merciful God, that I may ardently desire, prudently examine, and perfectly fulfill those things that are pleasing to Thee, to the praise and glory of Thy Holy Name. Amen.

AMDG

The following list of specific duties, considered to be the "indispensable minimum" expected of all Catholics, comes from the *Catechism of the Catholic Church* (#2042–2043):

1. "You shall attend Mass on Sundays and holy days of obligation."

2. "You shall confess your sins at least once a year."

3. "You shall humbly receive your Creator in Holy Communion at least during the Easter season."

4. "You shall keep holy the holy days of obligation."

5. "You shall observe the prescribed days of fasting and abstinence."

"The faithful also have the duty of providing for the material needs of the Church, each according to his abilities."

The works of art pictured in this book were specially chosen in order to edify as well as to provide visual illustrations of some of the most important doctrines of the Catholic faith. To this end, several reflection questions have been included below for each print that will help draw out its meaning. The prints in the text are numbered and listed according to the order in which they appear throughout the book.

COVER: *The Return of the Prodigal Son,* **Bartolome-Esteban Murillo; gift of the Avalon Foundation, © 1995 Board of Trustees, National Gallery of Art, Washington, D.C.**

1) Notice the clothing, posture, and facial expressions of the Prodigal Son. What do you think is running through his mind and heart? Whom do you think he represents?

2) What is the father doing? Whom do you think he represents?

3) What items are being brought into the picture by the servants? Why? (see Luke 15:11–32)

4) Why do you think the artist included the little dog in the picture?

5) How do you suppose the verse "the truth will set you free" (John 8:32) fits with this scene?

6) Which person(s) would you describe as "free" in this picture? How so? Why?

PRINT #1: *Our Lady of Sorrows* **statue (provided courtesy of the Basilica of the National Shrine of the Immaculate Conception, Washington, D.C.)**

1) Read John 19:17–42. Why do you think Mary has been given the title "Mother of Sorrows?"

2) How would you describe Mary's facial expression in this statue?

3) Have you prayed to Mary for help and support when in sorrow? When?

PRINT #2: *Christ the Teacher* icon (provided courtesy of the Basilica of the National Shrine of the Immaculate Conception, Washington, D.C.)

1) How did the iconographer portray Christ's right hand?

2) What do the two Greek letters in the book Christ is holding mean? (see Rev. 22:13)

3) Why do you suppose there is a halo around the head of Christ?

4) Does Christ still teach us today? How so?

PRINT #3: *Christ in Majesty* mosaic (provided courtesy of the Basilica of the National Shrine of the Immaculate Conception, Washington, D.C.)

1) What do you think the three flames around the head of Christ represent?

2) What does Christ's facial expression say to you?

3) Where are the three wounds on Christ's body, as it is pictured?

4) What is the color of Christ's robe? What do you suppose this signifies?

PRINT #4: *St. Peter Freed from Prison by an Angel*, Raphael (detail) (from Art Resources, New York)

1) Read Acts 12:1–19. Why was Peter in prison?

2) Notice how Peter is chained inside the cage. In what other ways can people be shackled or imprisoned, besides physically?

3) What part of the print is the lightest and brightest? Why do you suppose Raphael did this?

4) Why do you suppose the artist gave the angel wings? Where do you think the angel is pointing? Why?

PRINT #5: *Our Lady of Perpetual Help* mosaic (provided courtesy of the Basilica of the National Shrine of the Immaculate Conception, Washington, D.C.)

1) Where is Jesus looking in this picture?

2) What are the two angels pictured holding?

3) How is Our Lady "helping" Jesus in this picture?

4) How has Mary helped you in the past?

PRINT #6: *The Tabernacle in the Blessed Sacrament Chapel* (provided courtesy of the Basilica of the National Shrine of the Immaculate Conception, Washington, D.C.)

1) Why do you think this tabernacle is decorated so beautifully?

2) What do the golden pieces above the tabernacle signify? (see Exodus 16)

3) How often do you visit the tabernacle in your parish church?

4) Read #1378–1381 in the *Catechism of the Catholic Church*. Some have described being in the presence of Christ under the appearance of bread in the tabernacle as "a small foretaste of heaven." How is this so?

5) Why do you think this picture was chosen to be placed last in this book?

If you would like to order more copies of *The Truth Will Set You Free*, send $6.95 plus $3 postage and handling to:

Veritas Press
PO Box 89502
Sioux Falls, SD 57105–9055

or call:

1–800–705–3367

(VISA® and Master Card® accepted)

A complete and handy Teacher Manual, cross–referenced with the new *Catechism of the Catholic Church*, is also available ($20 plus $3 postage and handling).